# A JOURNAL *for* CAT LOVERS

**Illustrations by Melanie Lofland Gendron**
**Words by Elaine Goldman Gill**

The Crossing Press
Freedom, California  95019

Copyright © 1990 by The Crossing Press

Cover art and interior illustrations by Melanie Lofland Gendron

Printed in the U.S.A.

ISBN 0-89494-432-4

We found our first cat, or rather she found us, on upper Broadway in Manhattan. She curled around our legs repeatedly, saying "take me," "take me." We did take her back to our apartment, but unfortunately neither of us knew anything about cats. When we saw evidence of tapeworm, we struggled with two opposing ideas. Would we put her back on the street? Would we take her to a vet?

We took her to a vet who charged us what we thought was a lot of money (we were very poor) and, somehow, after we had paid his bill, we officially owned her. We proceeded to name her and to read books on how to take care of her.

Her name was Susie. She was a blue-grey, very elegant, very nervous alley cat. I was a smart graduate student but knew very little about anything besides books. Susie taught me a lot. I took her on walks thinking she'd be pleased—she was terrified. I've never understood the people who take cats out on leashes. They are totally at the mercy of any dog passing by. The point is, if you have a cat, it's important to get inside her skin, to imagine what it's like to be her. After all, it's not unlike having human friends or learning to live with someone.

Later on, we got another cat called Felix, a big orange tom, who loved to stare out the window at the pigeons (we were on the 5th floor) and make clucking sounds in the back of his throat and whip his tail around, in ecstasy of anticipation.

I saw them mate, saw Susie get pregnant, and give birth. I looked on and sweated it through with her. The babies were beautiful and the sound of her purring in the closet where she was nursing was wonderful. I felt like a grandmother, cuddling every kitten, protective of them as though they were my own. I found all of this useful when I gave birth to my own children.

Susie lived a full eighteen years, and since that time I have never gone without a cat, except now, when our last cat was hit by a car and died a few months thereafter. I've sworn that while I live on a busy street, I'll not have another cat. I'll wait until we move to a safer place, but it's hard. A cat is the heart of any house.

*Elaine Goldman Gill*

Children make up the best names for cats: One-Eyed Brown (he had both eyes OK and wasn't brown), Sherpa (he looked like someone from Tibet), Tamar —The Abyssinian Queen of the East, Tolley (short for Ptolemy), Sanchez, and Thrasher.

When you first bring a cat or kitten home, it's nice to show the cat her sleeping place, a box lined with something woolly that you would otherwise throw away, something that has your smell on it. And it's best to introduce her to the litter box (she will get the idea).

The best way to show your cat that you love her is to wet your hand slightly and run it over her fur, head to toe. This is a simulation of a mother cat licking her baby. It works. You will adopt the cat and the cat will adopt you.

When you meet a cat you don't know, proceed cautiously. Put your hand out for her to sniff. If she doesn't look anxious, proceed to stroke her whiskers gently back towards her cheeks.

Cats will greet you nose to nose, if you are on their level. They greet each other the same way. Dogs do it nose to rear. I have never understood why.

A piece of noisy cellophane tied around the middle with a four foot piece of string is a wonderful plaything for a cat. Wriggle the "butterfly" in the air and on the floor, and watch the cat's response.

Another great toy is a scrap of fur tied around the middle with a piece of string. You can simulate a mouse zig-zagging across a floor.

Have you tried moving your hand under a blanket, pretending it's a mouse hiding underneath? You know how a cat will pounce on your toes under the blanket—your hand is much more mobile than your foot.

Cats like to scratch to sharpen their claws. Either have something that is OK to scratch, an old chair you plan to recover some day, or buy a scratching post.

A scratching post is easy to make. You'll need a heavy square of wood or a thinner square that can be bolted down (to make the gadget stable), and a log or thick dowel covered with a square of carpet (a carpet sample should be fine).

Some people advise a horizontal scratch box, rather than a vertical one. I've watched cats on their hind legs scratching at trees. I'd vote for the vertical one.

I'd never declaw a cat. She would be totally without defenses. You should provide your cat with a proper place to scratch and tell her in no uncertain terms what you want her to do. Or you can let your cat go outside to scratch on trees.

If your cat repeatedly goes after your good chair, tape aluminum foil over whatever portion is being scratched. This should stop her in her tracks.

Some people advise keeping an old Windex bottle filled with plain water. Spray the cat when she's doing something you don't like. Obviously, you have to catch the cat in the act. Otherwise, the punishment has no meaning. I really don't like this sort of punishment but have no doubt it works.

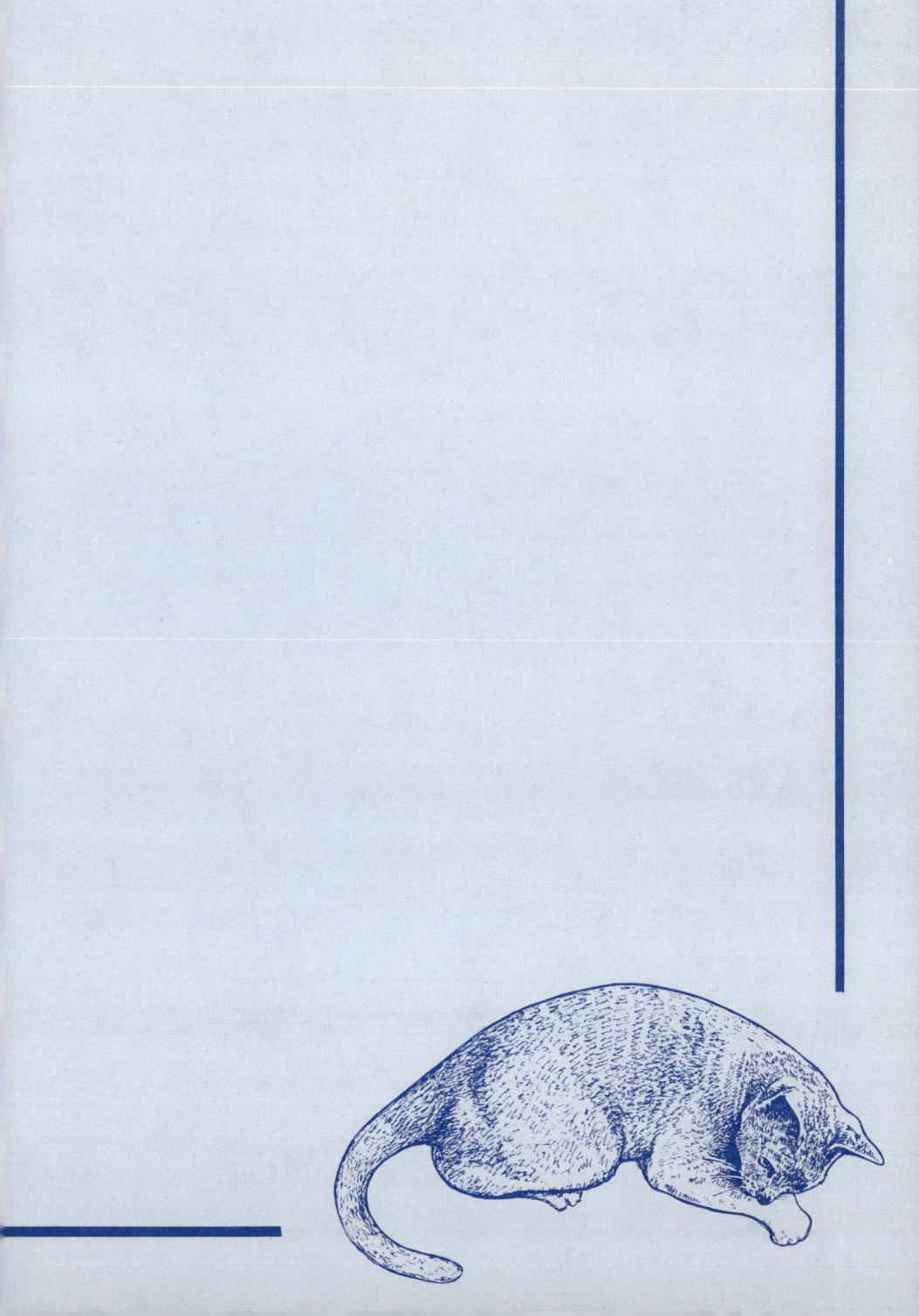

If you let a cat go outside, how do you know when she wants to go outside? Simple. She will generally stand at the door and look at you expectantly.

How do cats signal to get let in? Mine either leaped four paws worth on the screen door and yowled, or scratched vigorously on the glass door, or simply yowled. The communication is easy.

I've had cats who were outside in the yard in the morning make a run for the door as soon as they heard the snap of blinds being pulled up.

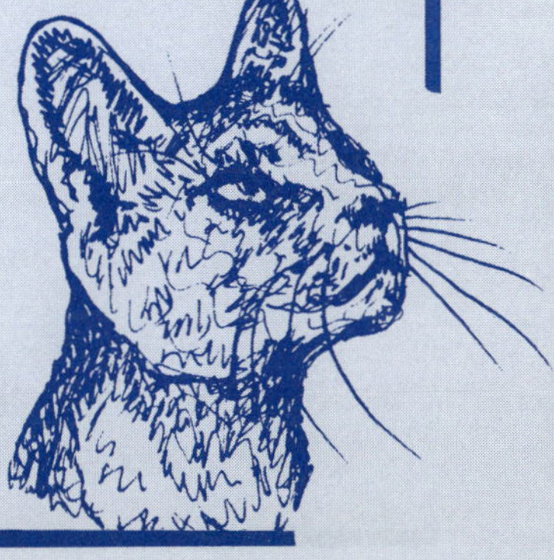

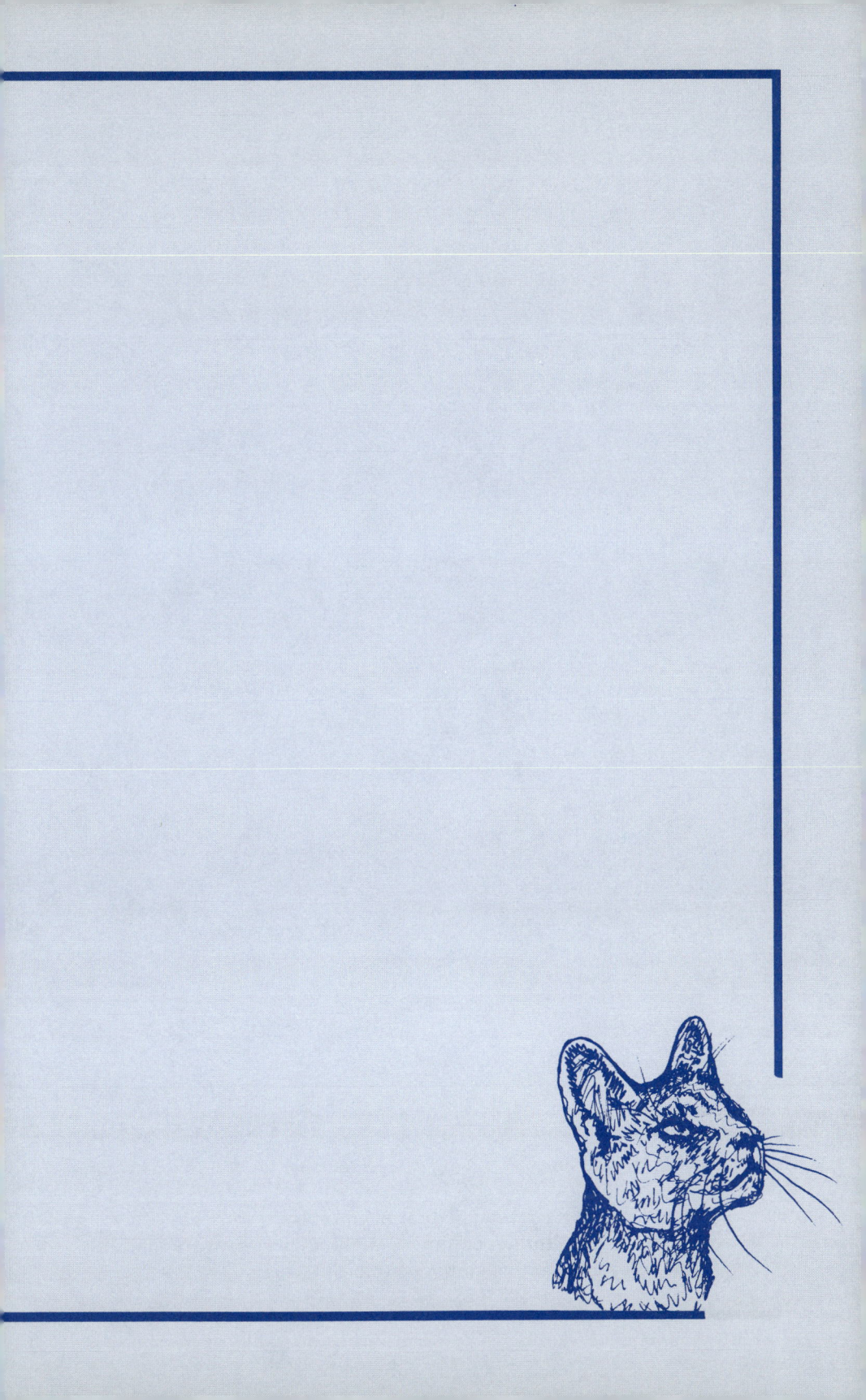

You can, of course, cut a small door in your big door so that you don't have to monitor her coming and going, but be aware that you may get some unwelcome visitors this way.

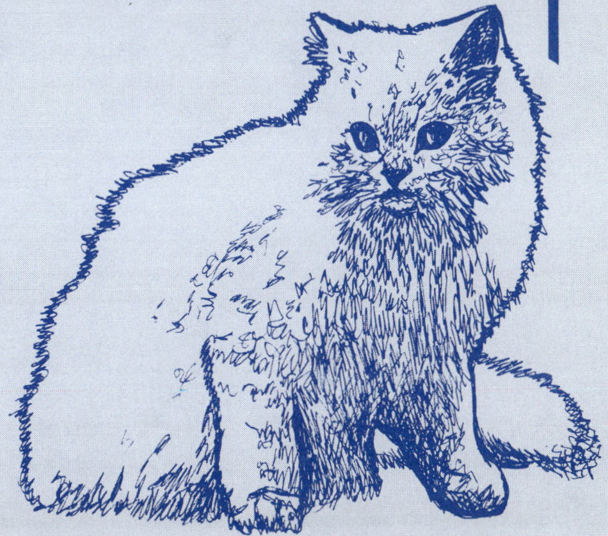

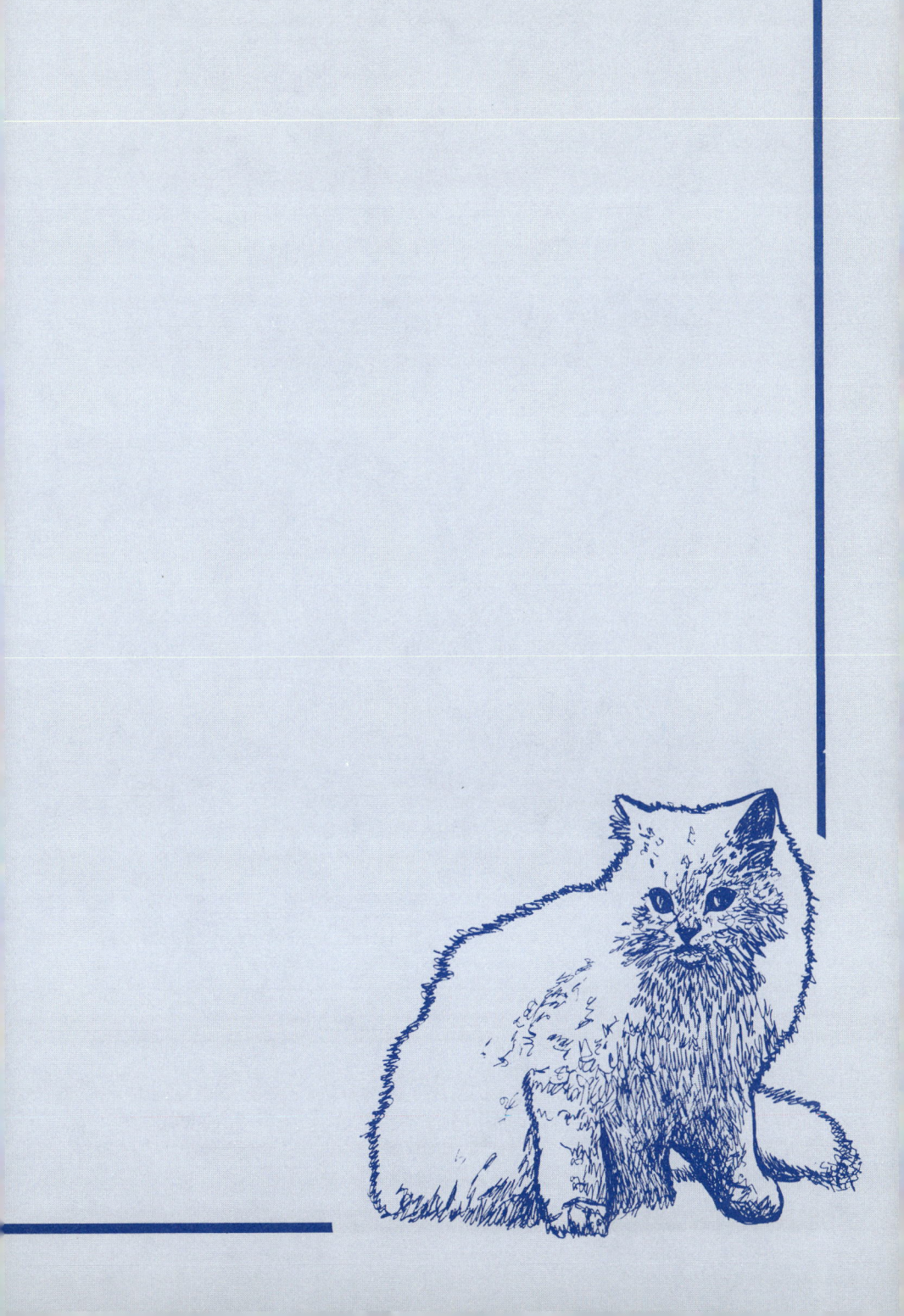

One woman I know has a simple arrangement. The cat sleeps all day in the house. At night she goes out and stays out all night. There's no need for a litter box this way.

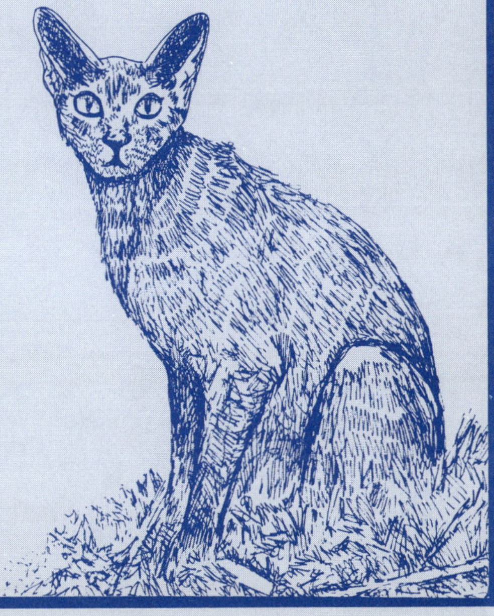

If a cat isn't allowed outside, you'll need a litter box. If you have a shovel and a backyard, you can use earth—it's free. And if you don't feed your cat dried cat food containing preservatives, you can dump the contents of the dirty box back in the compost heap.

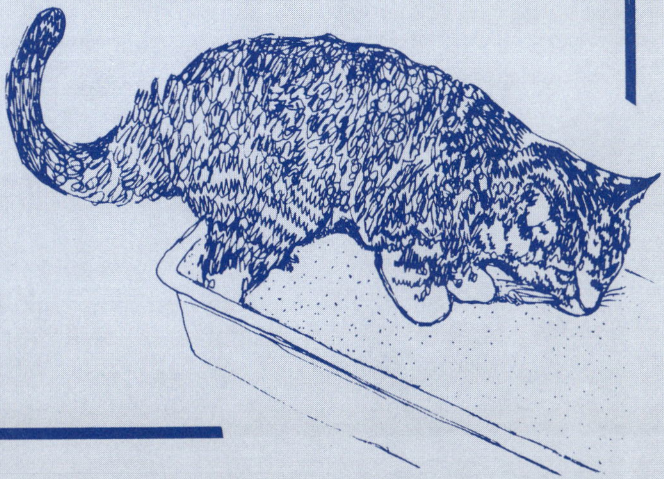

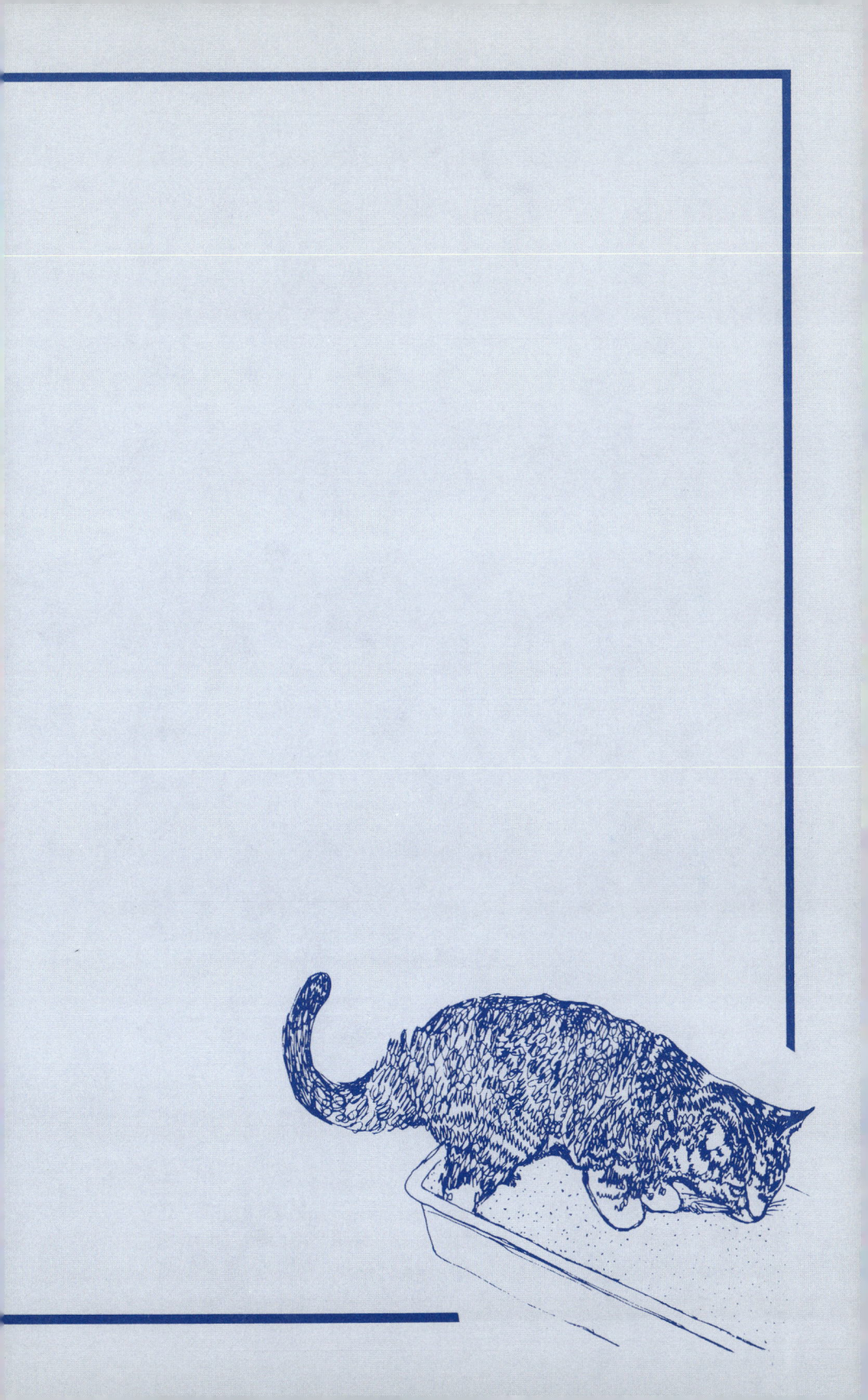

If you don't have a backyard, use commercial cat litter. A nice tip—sprinkle baking soda on the bottom of your dry, clean box before adding the litter. It will help absorb odors.

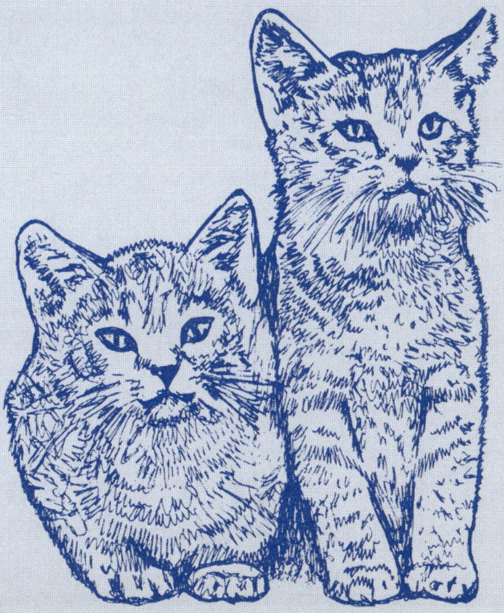

Incidentally, you don't have to buy a cat box. Any cardboard box big enough to contain the cat will do—just line it with plastic (a garbage bag is fine).

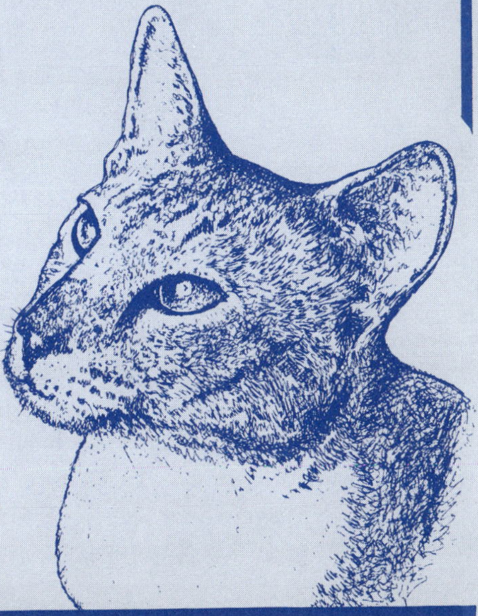

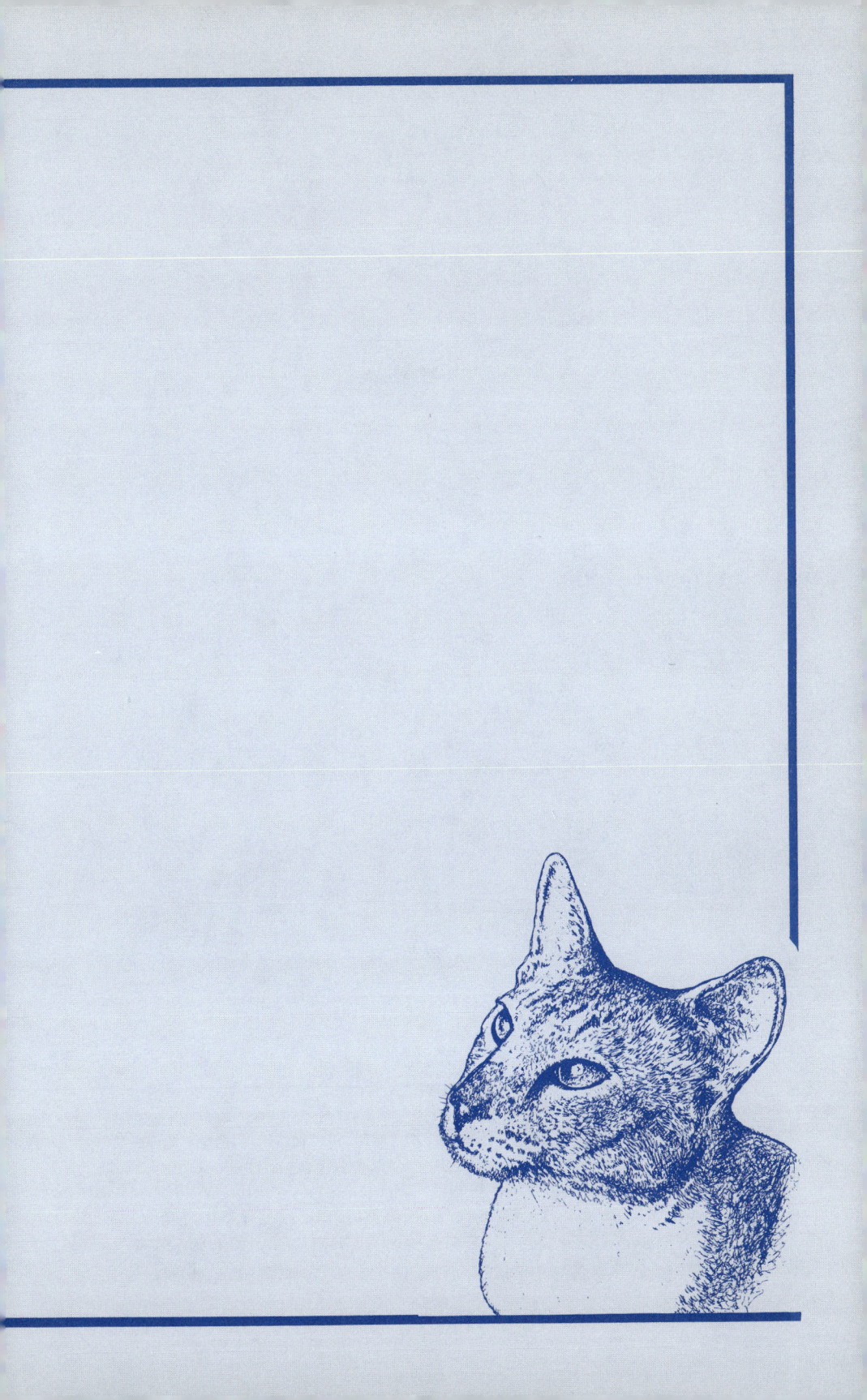

Some people teach their cats to use the toilet. It's hard and will take time. You have to get the cat used to a toilet seat on top of a litter box, and then you have to get the cat used to using the toilet seat on the toilet itself. The trick is to start the cat on a spare seat on top of the litter box, and then raise the seat with two-by-fours or bricks slowly to the heights of a real toilet. Then remove the litter box and spare seat. You'll have to remember to keep the top of your toilet seat up all the time.

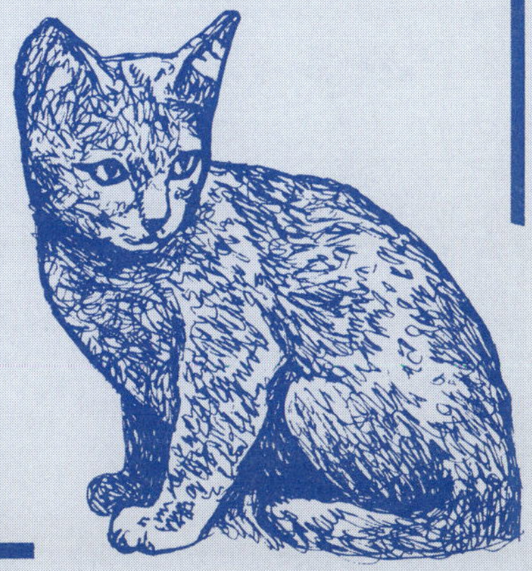

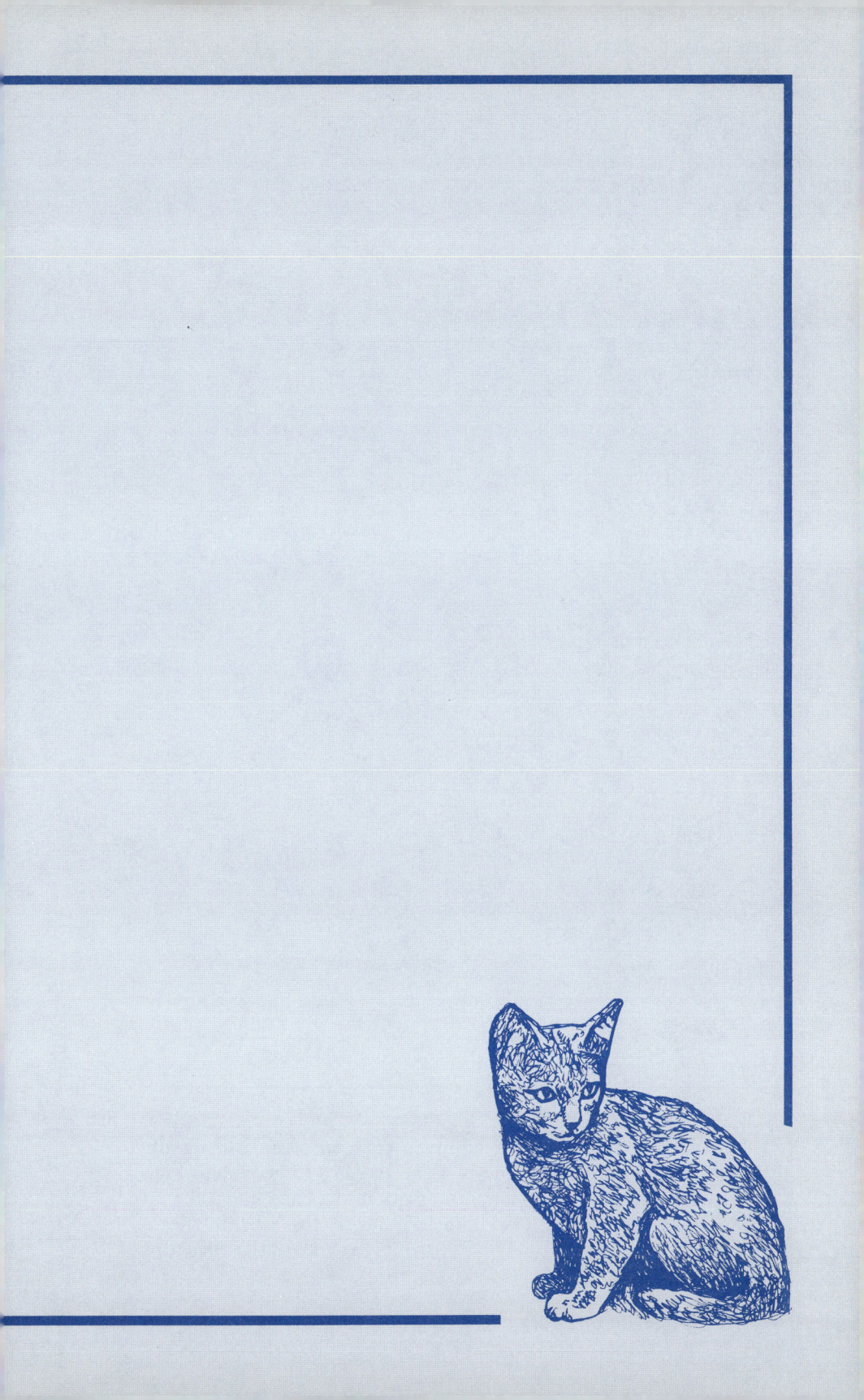

It's nice to have a place where a cat can sleep during the daytime. A sunny window is ideal. An empty bookshelf high off the ground with easy access is good too. Cats like to be up high and safe. They also like looking at the world from a vantage point, the same way birds like to stand at the very tops of trees.

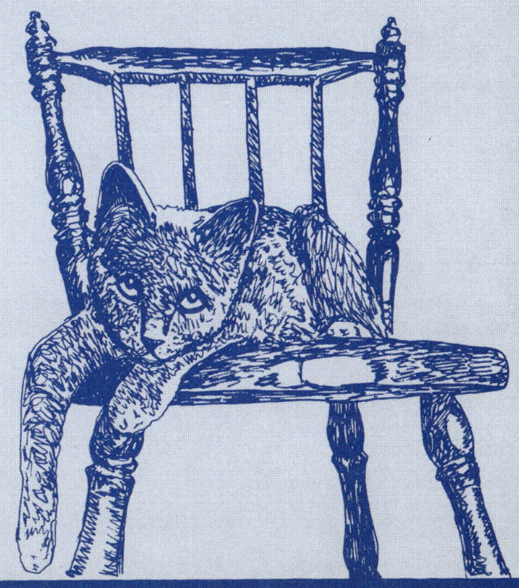

I've never had trouble with dogs and cats in the house. If necessary, they will walk around each other to avoid trouble, at worst. At best, they will love each other as much or more than they love you and the dog will groom the cat.

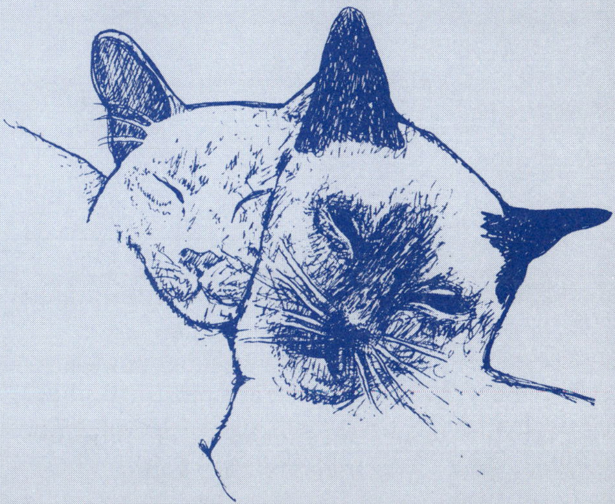

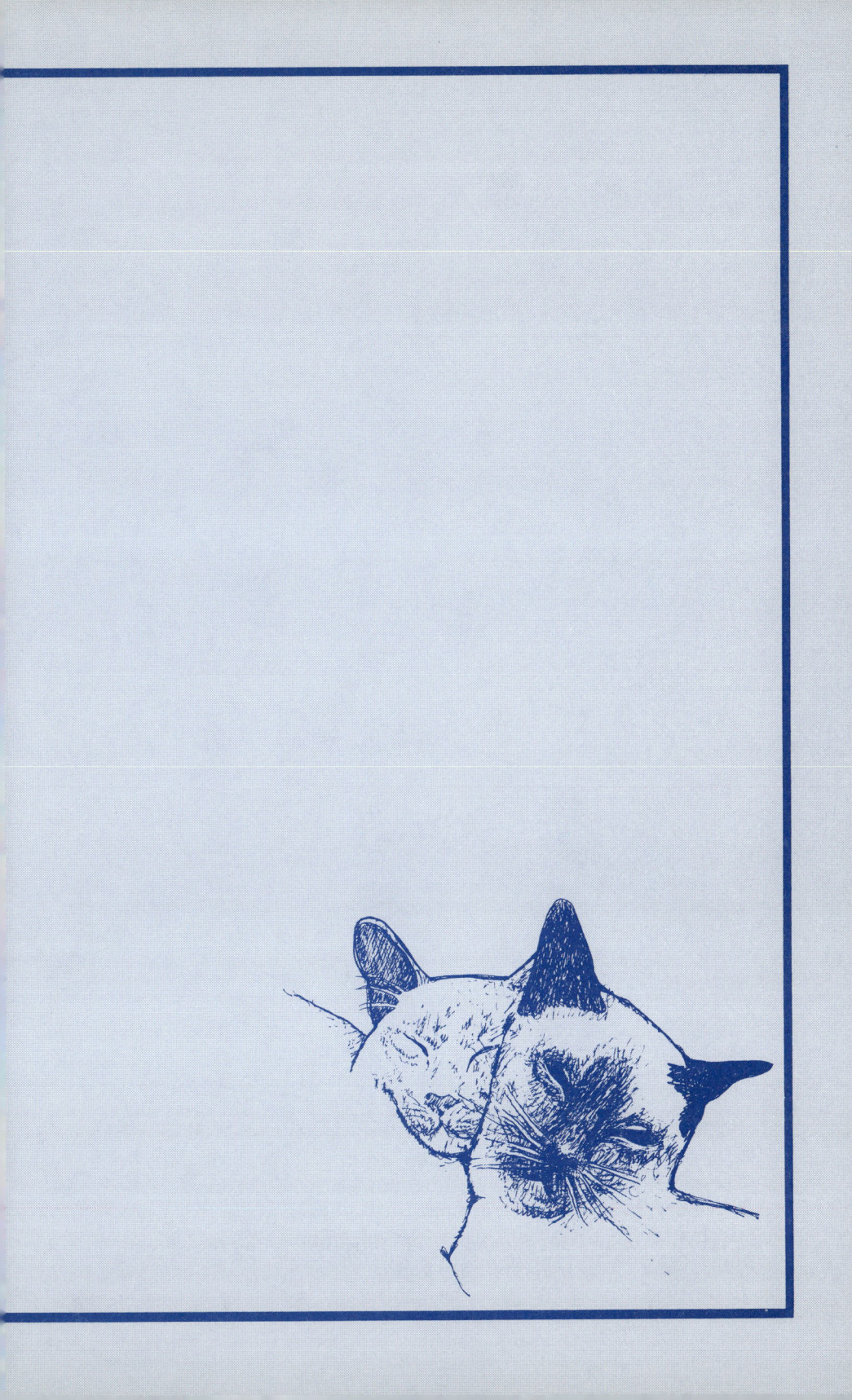

Probably the best arrangement is to introduce a dog to a cat or vice versa when they are both young.

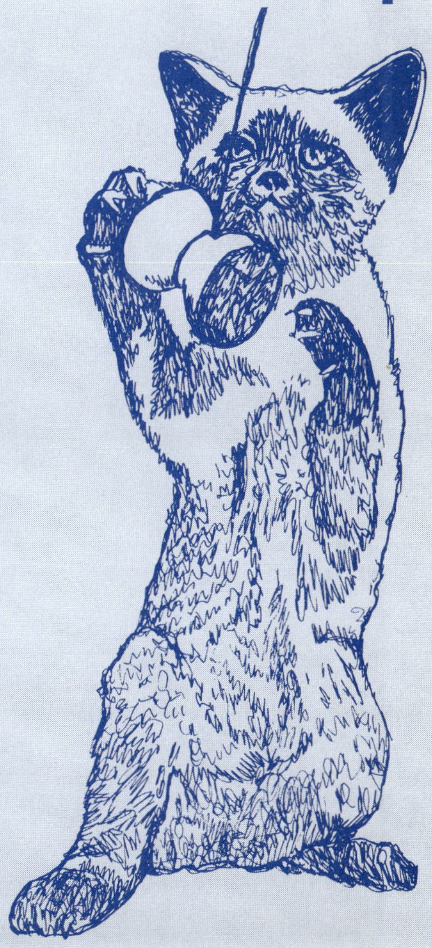

Sometimes, there will be a great aversion that you can't help. Tamar, our Abyssinian, couldn't stand a little white terrier called Willy and would torment him repeatedly by leaping on his back, claws extended. He solved the problem by not going near her. He'd check out every room carefully before he came in.

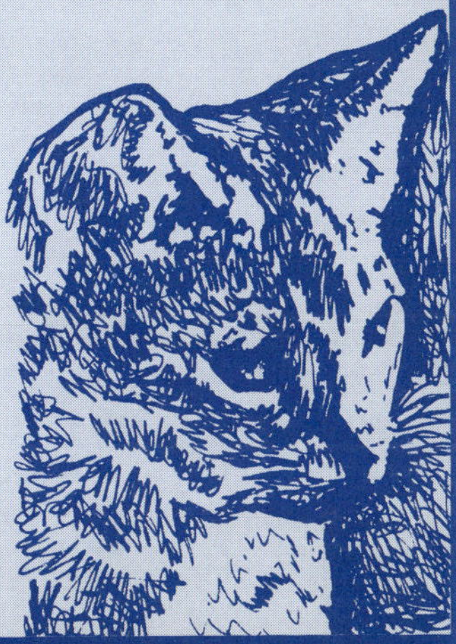

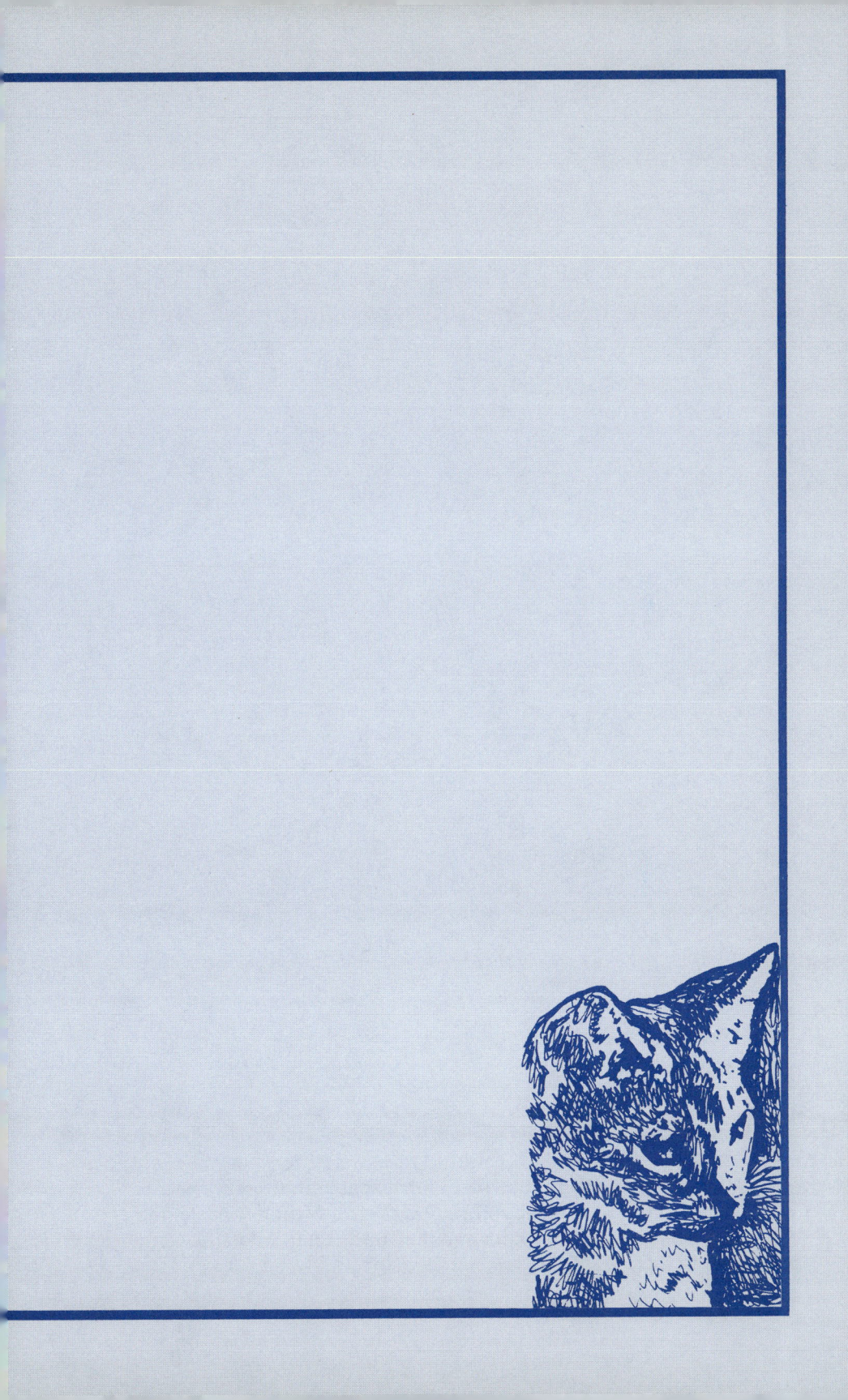

If you point at any object, a cat will look at your finger, whereas a dog will look at what you're pointing at. More precisely, the dog will look at your finger and then follow it to what you want him to look at.

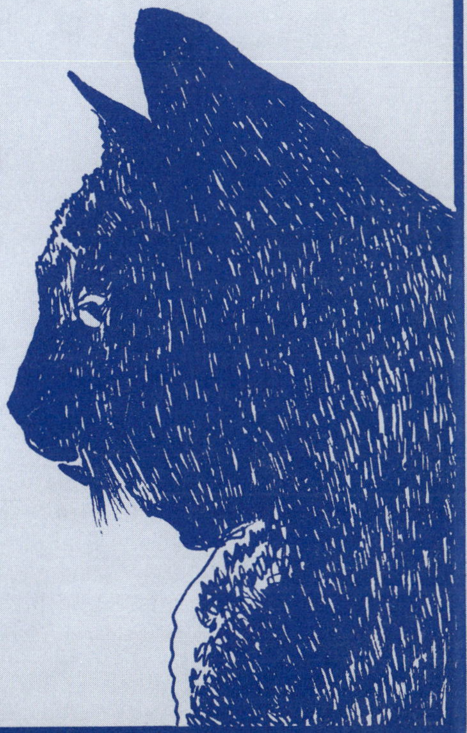

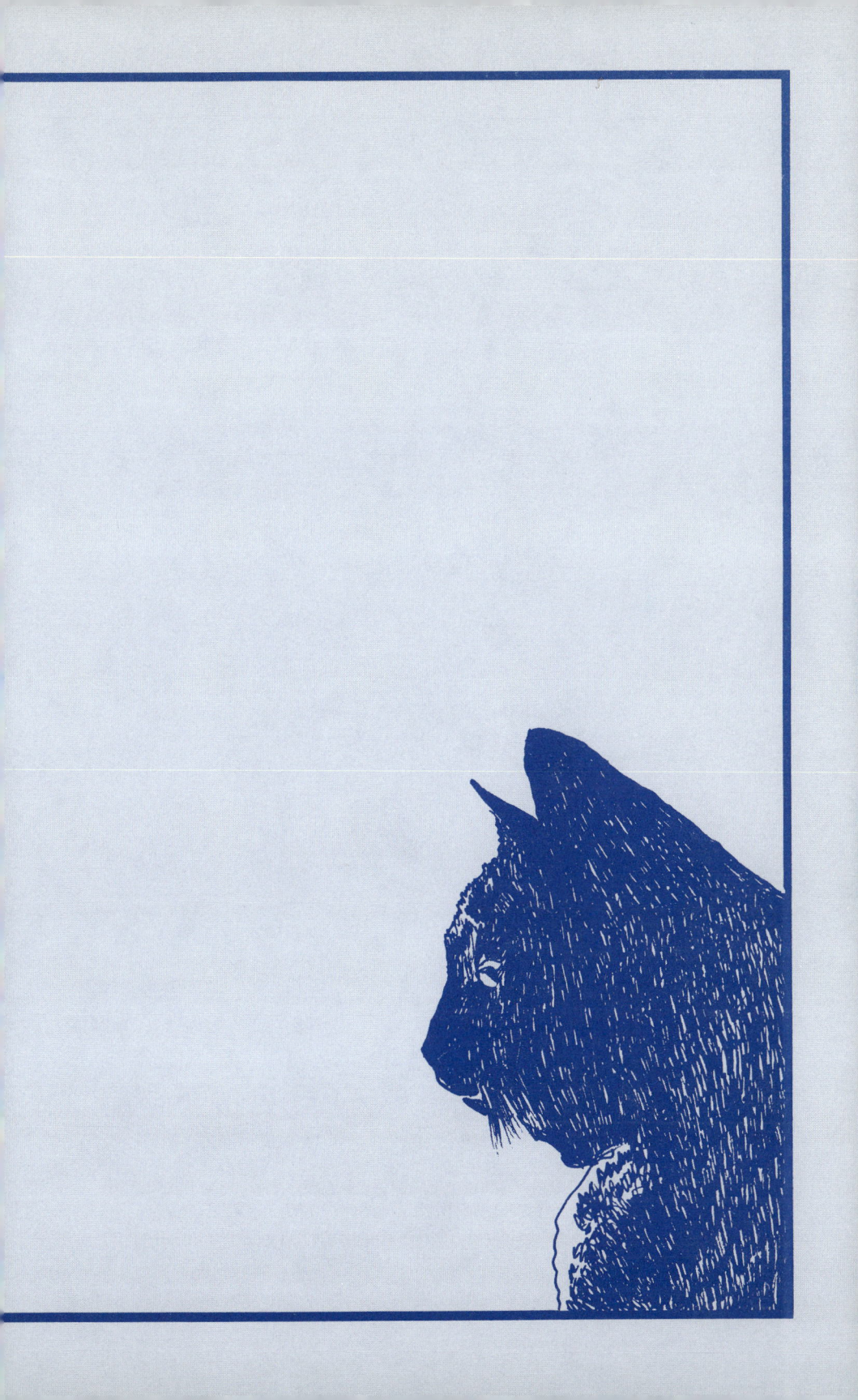

Some people like to sleep with cats on the bed. They do keep your feet warm. But be prepared—they may wake up earlier than you do.

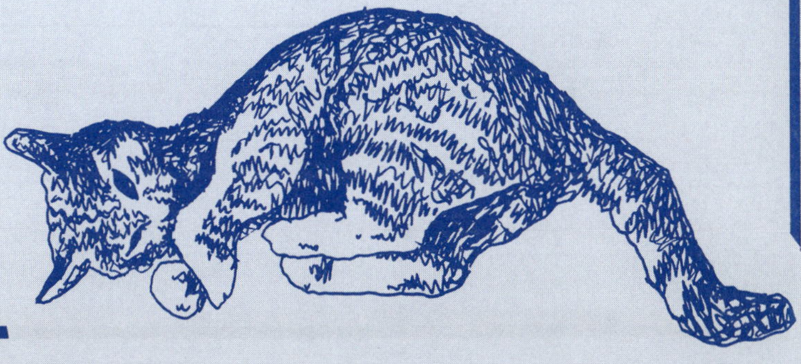

I've been awakened by cats curling around my face or licking my eyelids.

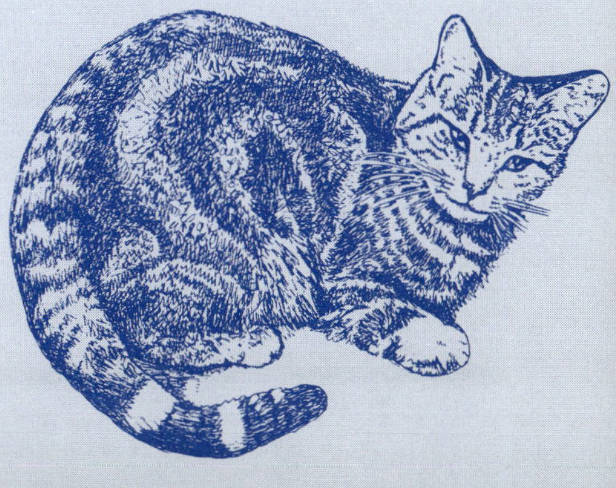

Cats will eat palm trees that you have in pots around the house. I don't know any solution—they like palm trees. You can try planting grass seed in an aluminum baking sheet with a thin level of dirt, or you could try catnip seed.

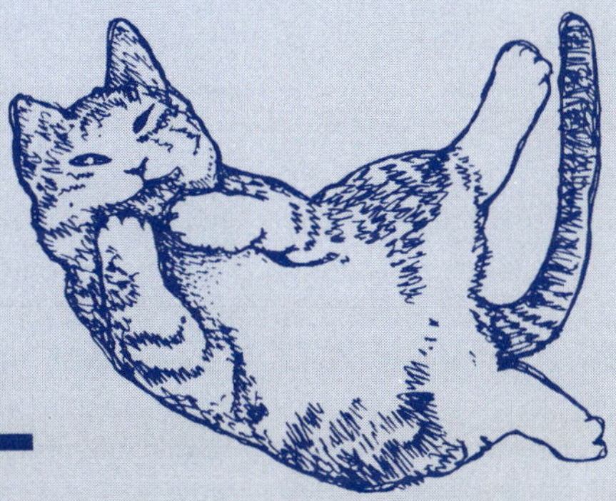

A small child has to be taught respect for a cat. It's not easy, but it can be done. Generally, a child is fascinated by anything furry that moves, so that part is easy. What's hard is to teach a child to handle a cat gently, and never, never pick it up by the back of the neck. All four paws have to be supported.

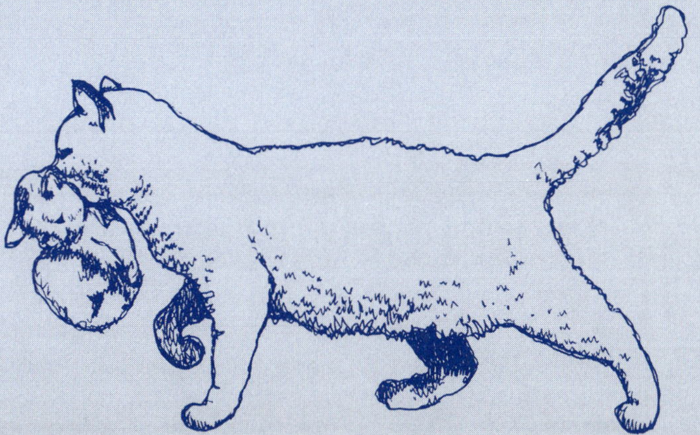

Some people advise cutting meat for a cat in small pieces. I don't know why. How, for instance, can she bite into a mouse she's caught? I think the work of biting into a biggish piece of meat is pleasurable, not easy, but worth doing, from the cat's point of view.

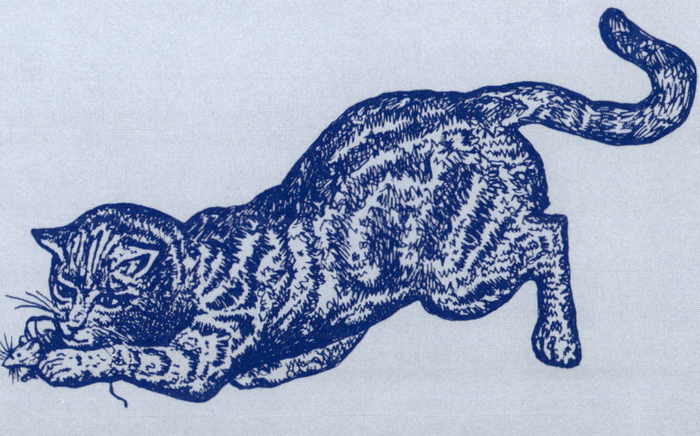

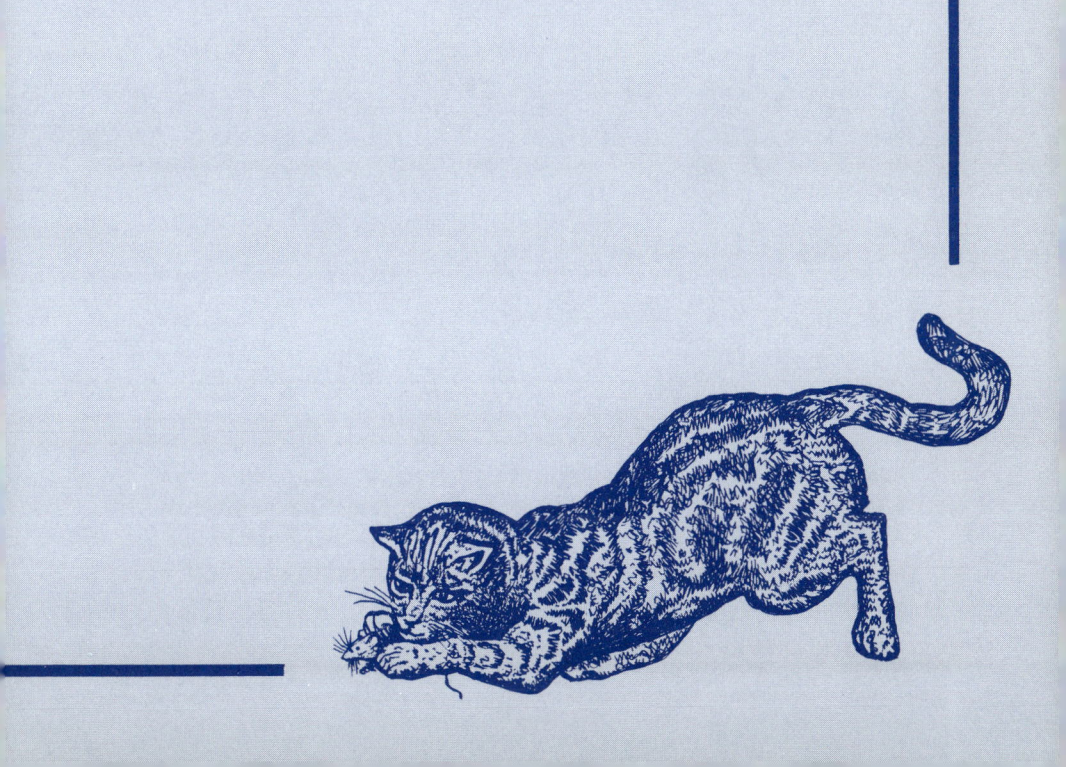

We've had male cats who weren't neutered. They'd come home with half their ears chewed off and deep bites that wouldn't heal. And they never lived beyond two to three years. I'd always alter a male. It's the only way I've found to keep him a reasonable time.

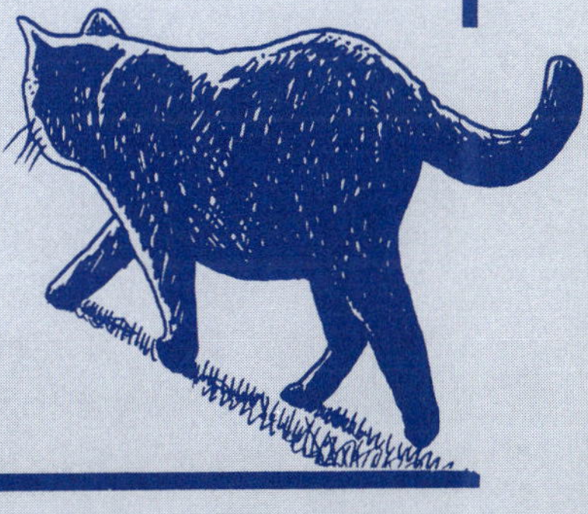

A tom who is not altered will spray—the smell is extremely penetrating. Of course it's simply his way of marking his territory. I understand it but wouldn't put up with it. Please alter your male cats.

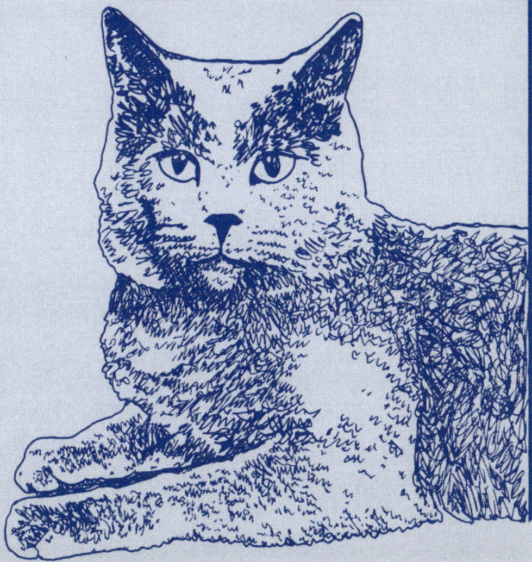

It's best to alter female cats too. The cat population is too high anyway, and the poor folks at the SPCA have to gas the ones that aren't wanted. It's best to stop it at the source, your female cat.

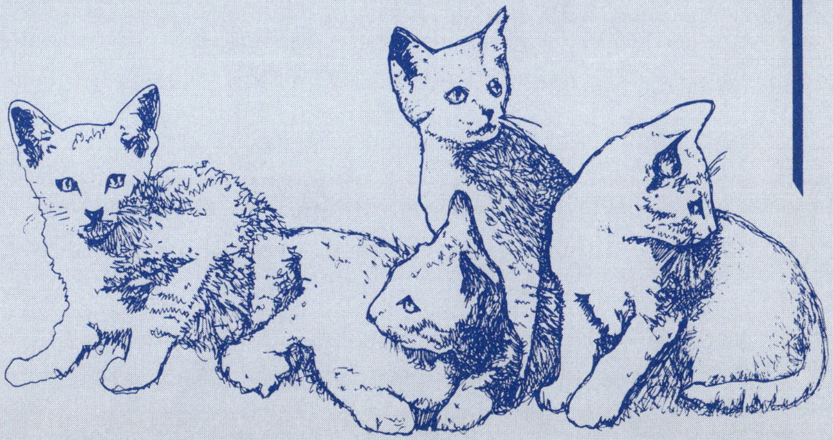

I have mated all the female cats we've had at least once. I thought they were better companions after they had babies. However, I personally saw to it that every one of the babies was adopted by good people, and that's a lot of work. If you're not up to it, don't do it.

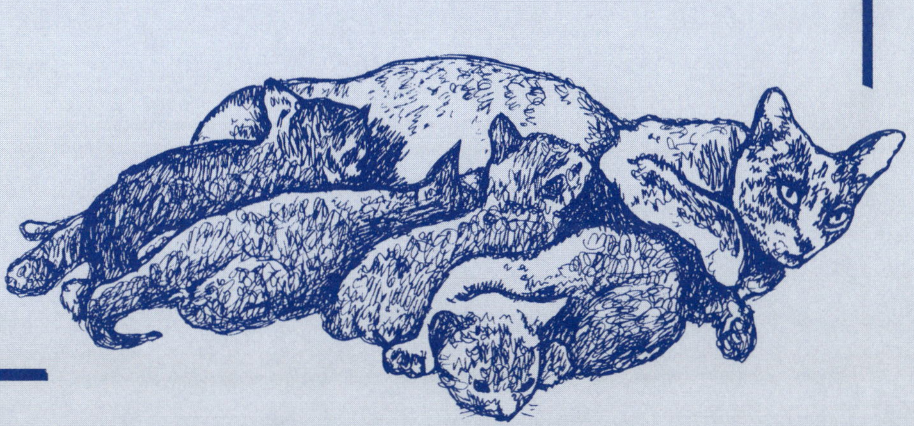

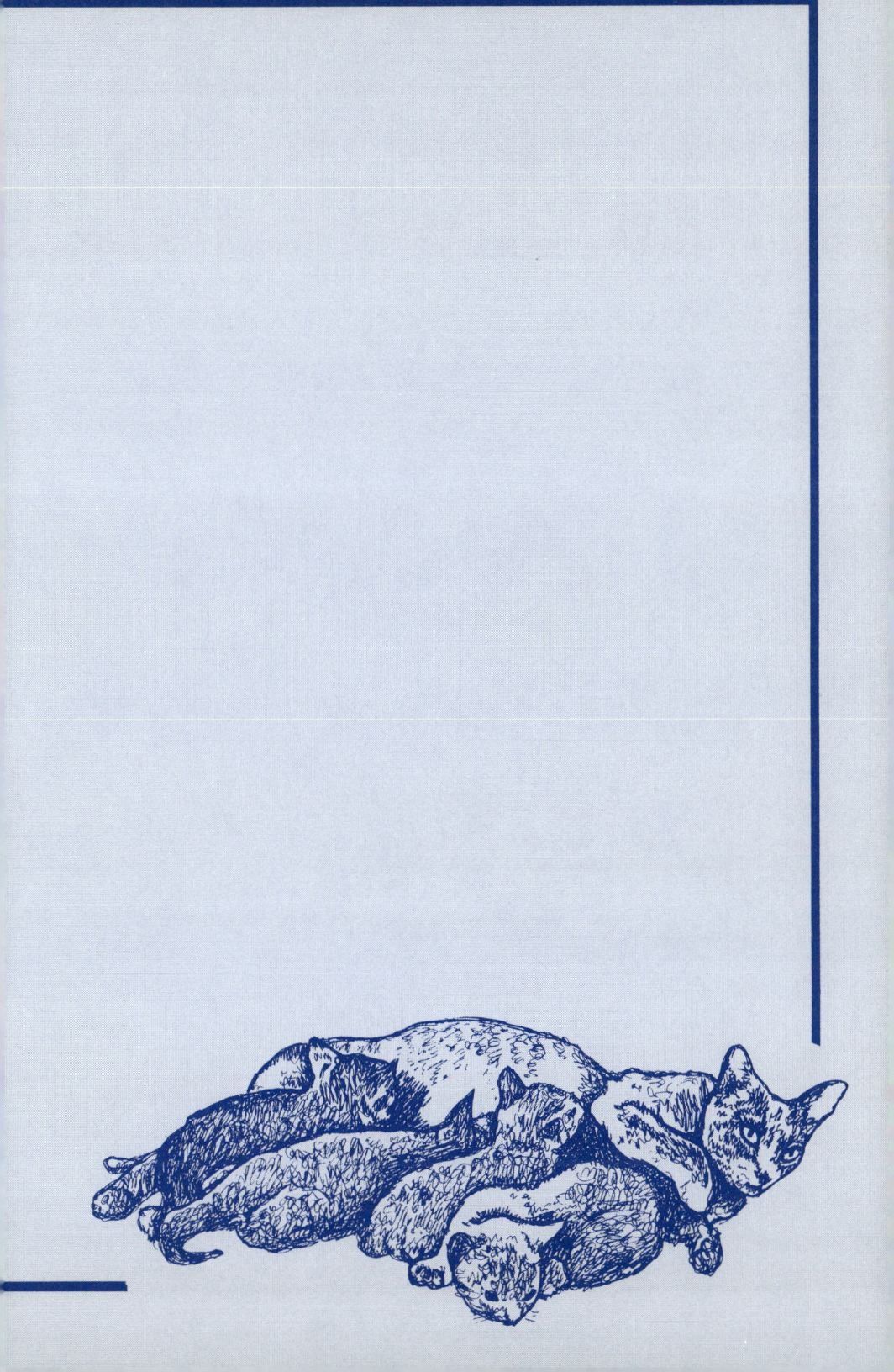

By the way, I never knew how to tell the difference between male and female kittens, until someone explained it to me: the females have a dot under their tails (the anus), and a slit below that (the vagina); the males have a dot under their tails (the anus) and a dot below that (the penis).

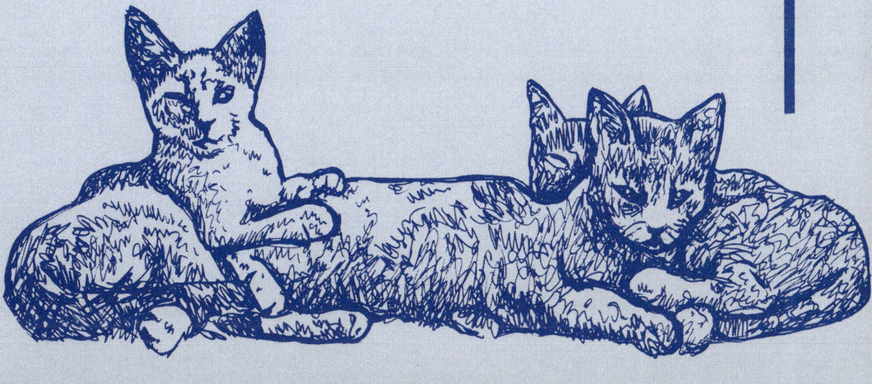

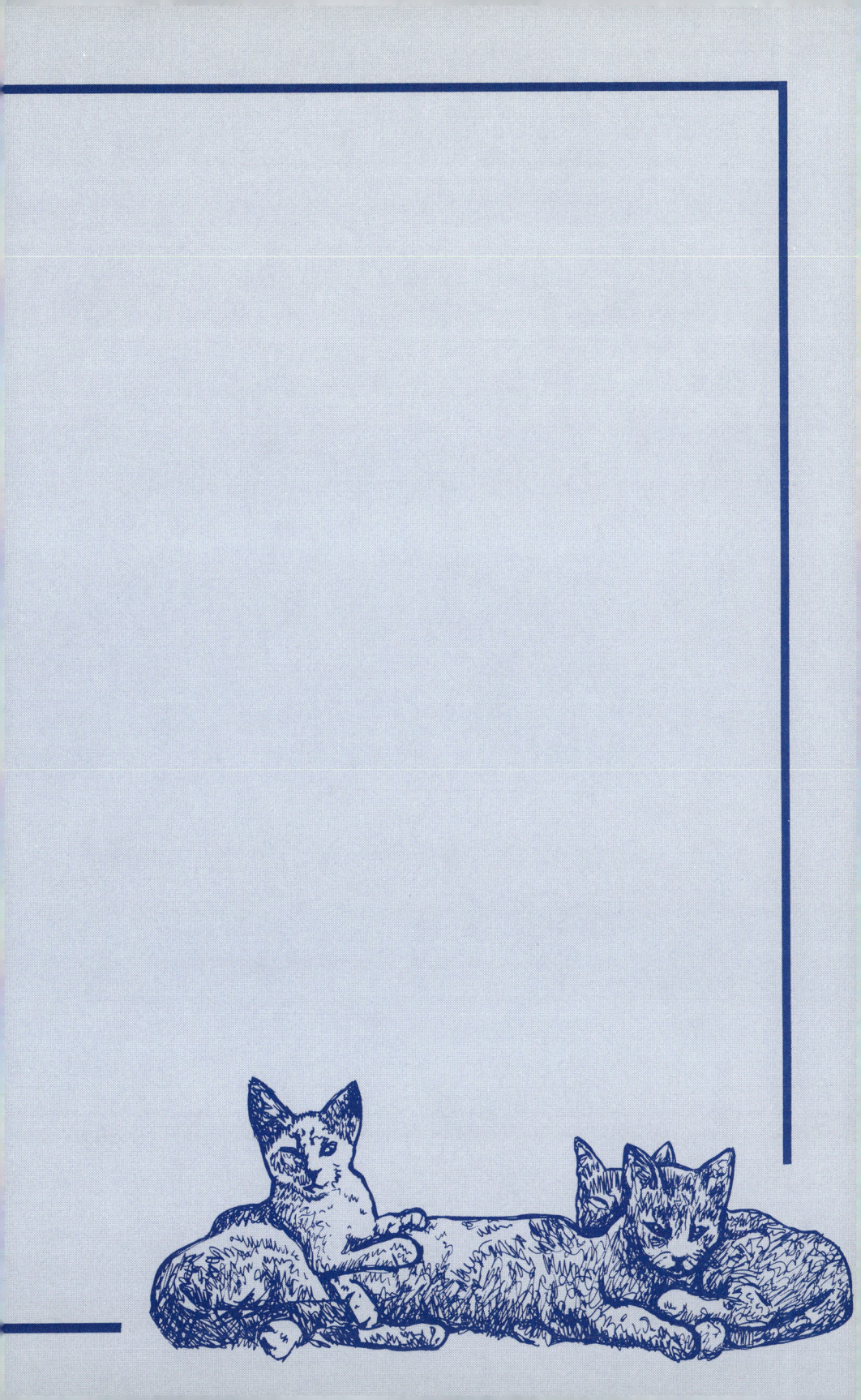

You should have no problem with fleas if your animal is healthy and routinely combed with a fine-toothed comb. You can periodically put the comb in a glass of alcohol or hot water to kill the fleas.

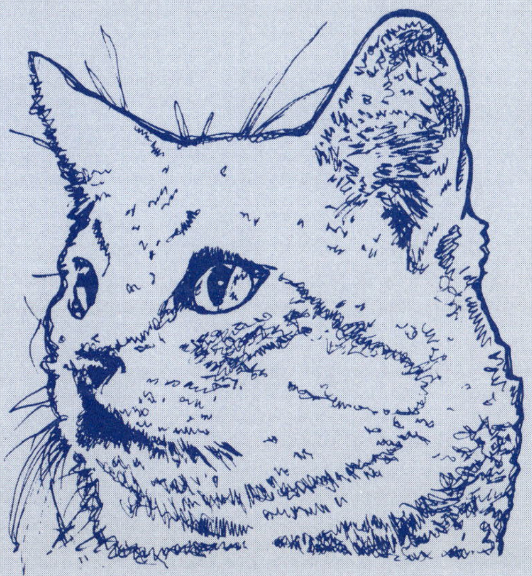

I wouldn't use flea collars because I consider them poisonous. The poison spreads from the neck to the cat and then onto your hands.

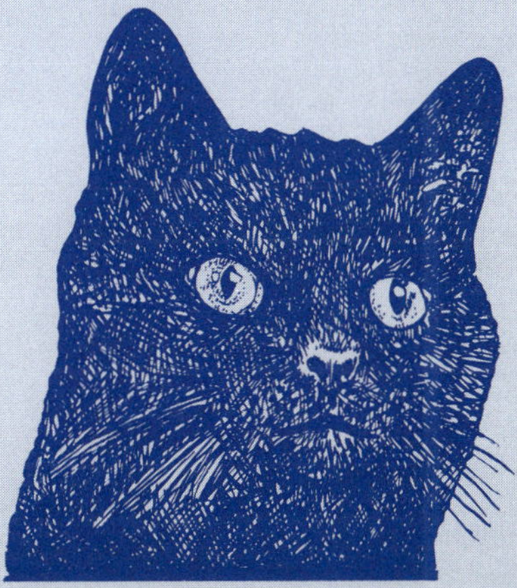

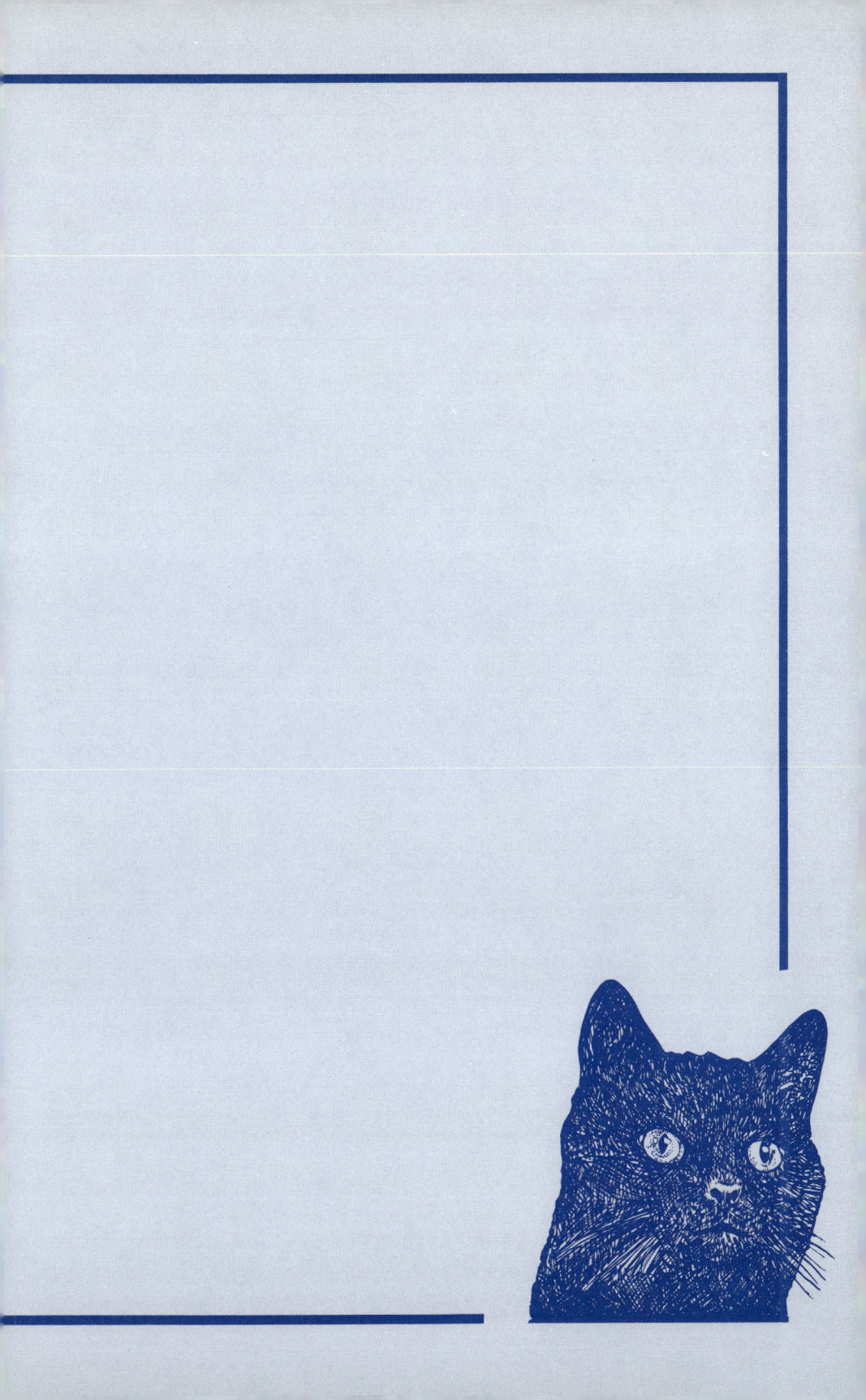

People say that brewer's yeast and garlic added to the cat's food help deter fleas. Can't hurt—at the least, these are healthful additions to your cat's diet.

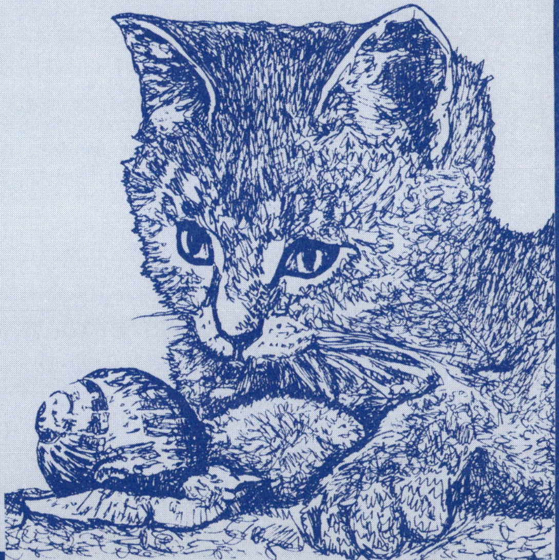

Of course, with so many cats in our household, we've had many deaths to cope with. When we had a country house, we'd bury the cats simply. We'd ask the children to contribute flowers and place them in the grave. If they were up to it, they could touch their dead pet in farewell. It eases the pain to have an appropriate ceremony.

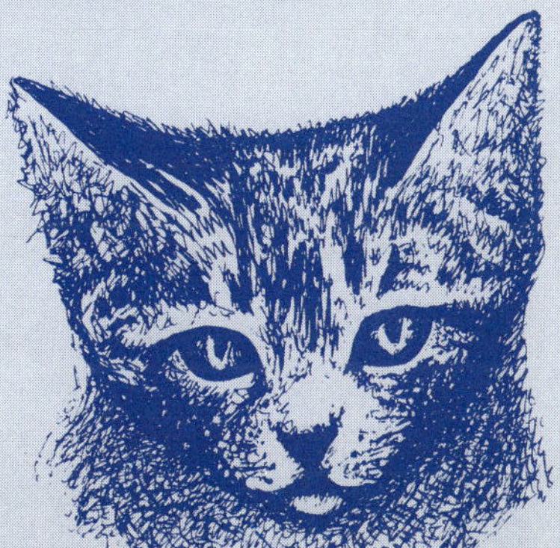

We let Sherpa die under the live oak tree in the backyard. The woman next door who loved him asked why we didn't let the vet do the job. I replied that he enjoyed himself in his last few days—I figured it was worth it to him.

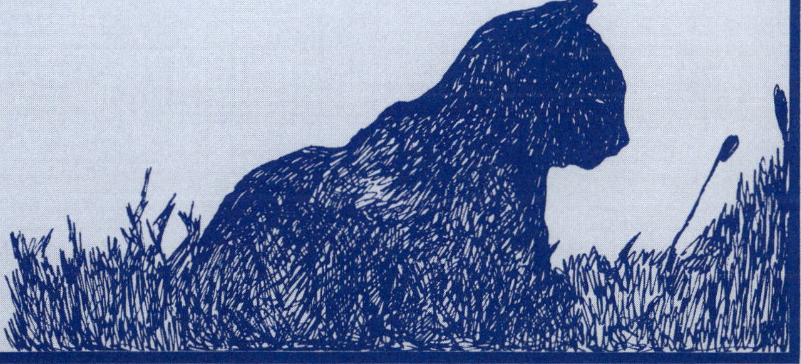

Even with a small backyard, I buried Sherpa and wept. It was good for me.

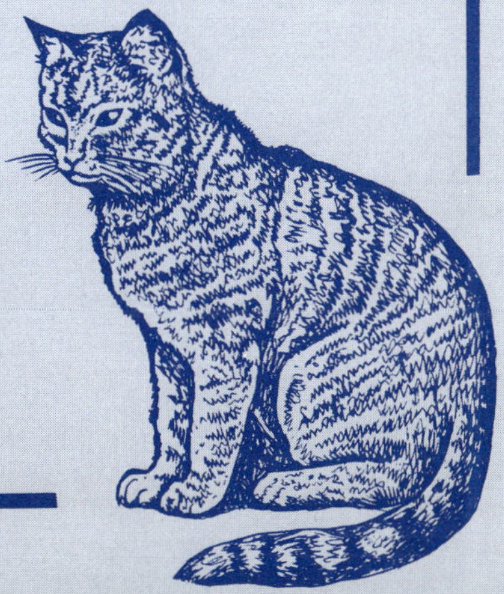

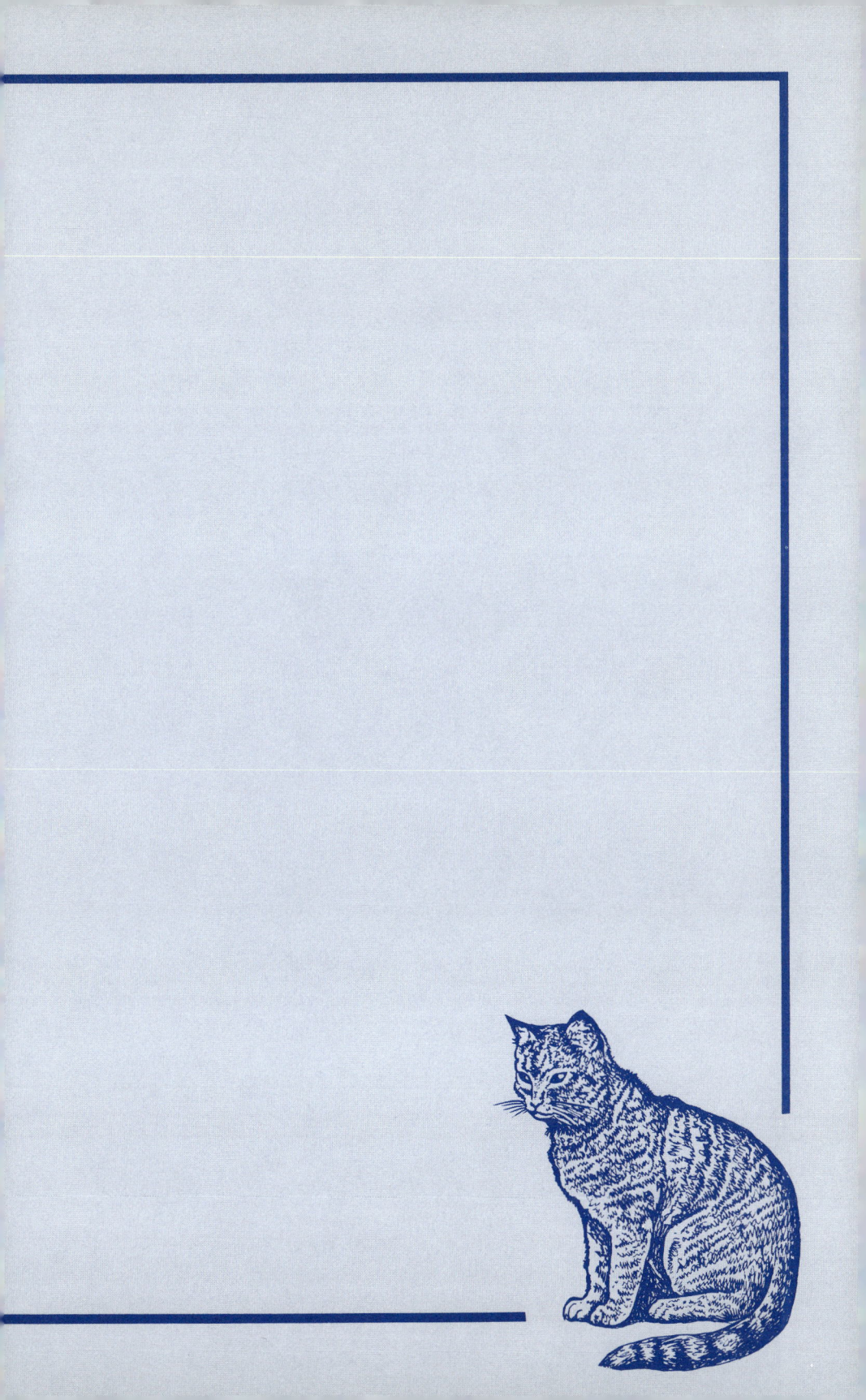

If you can't bury your cat, I'd urge you to take the cat to a vet for cremation. Ask for the ashes and sprinkle them on your roses or flower garden. Invite your children to take part in this ceremony.

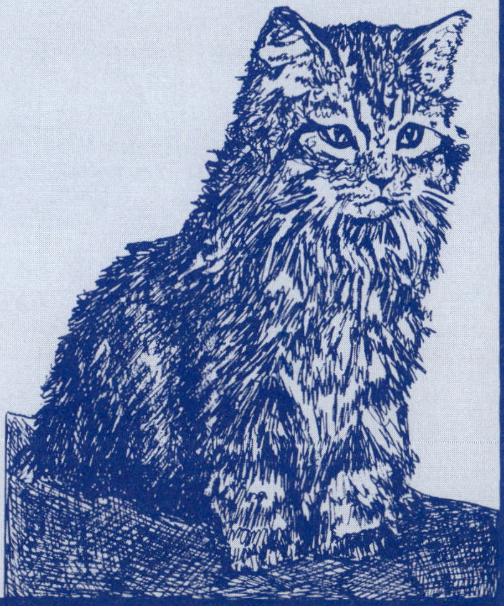

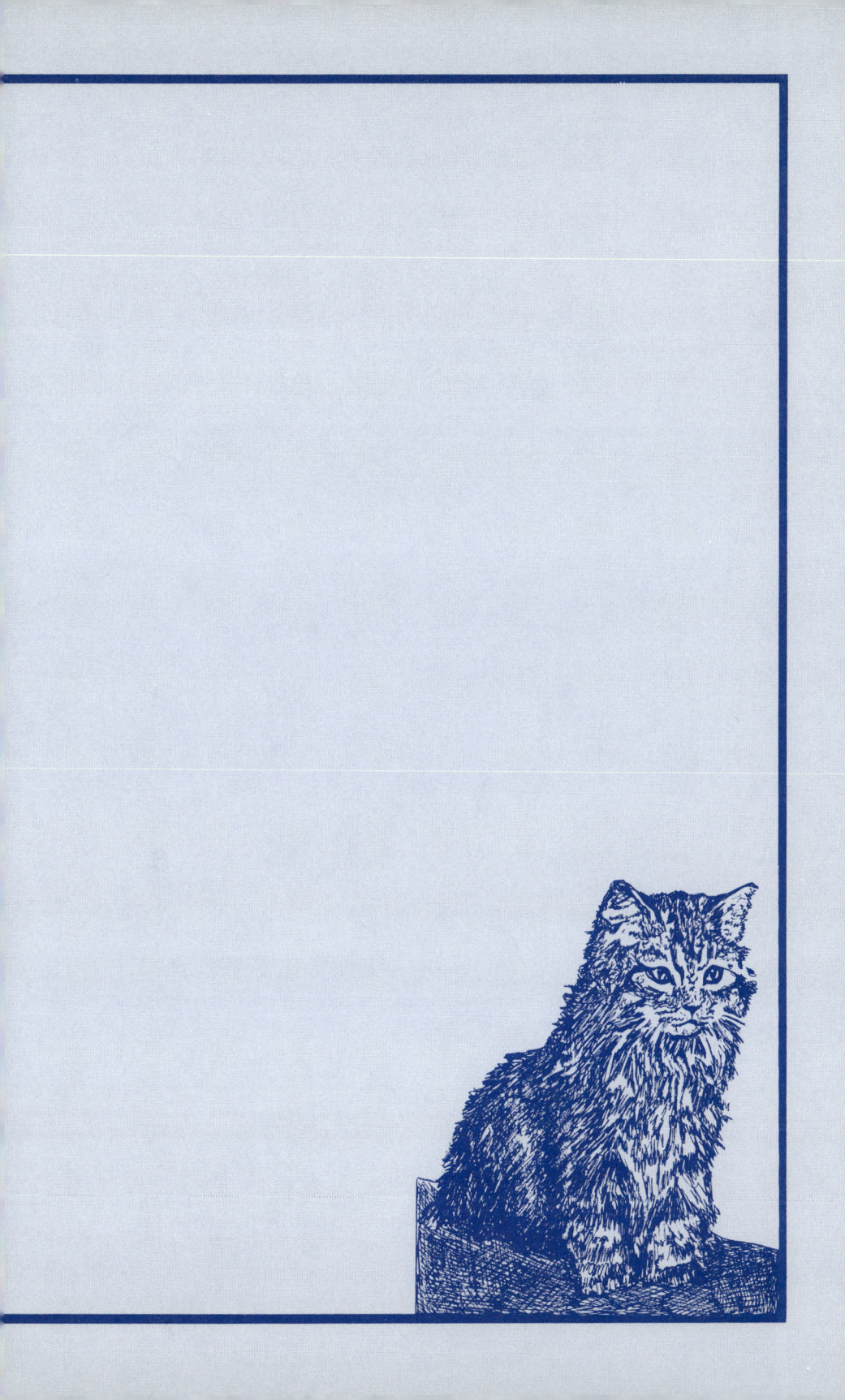

I have never put an animal "to sleep," except when it was hit by a car. Generally we have let the cat or dog take its time going out. One cat, Whitey, decided to die in a bathtub. It slowed up the baths for the household, but it was worth it to let her do her thing.

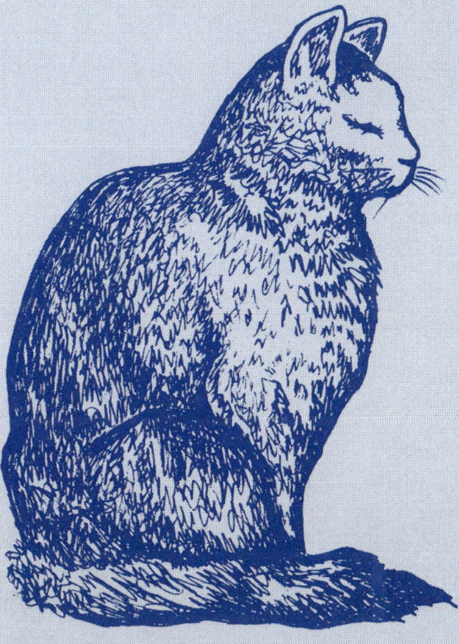

We fed our cats two times a day. If you use dry cat food, please try to get the best you can buy, without preservatives like BHA and BHT. We always keep a bowl of fresh water available.

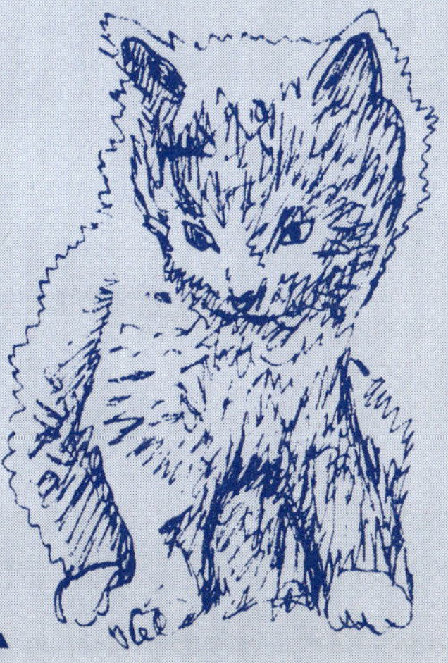

It is nice to vary dry cat food with fresh organ and muscle meats, or with canned cat food.

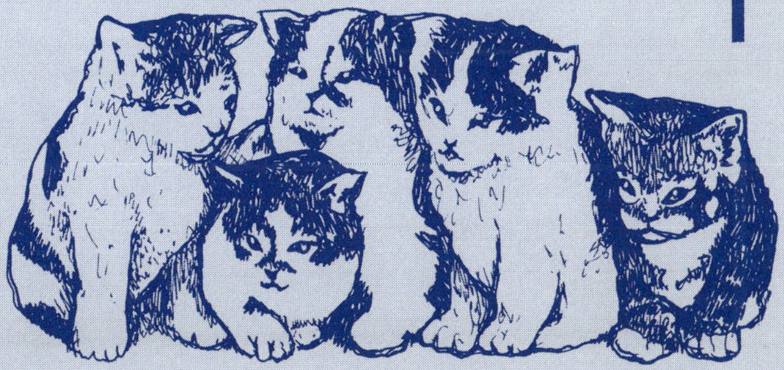

If you decide to go the whole way and cook from scratch for your cat, please get a good cookbook, like *Natural Health for Dogs and Cats*.

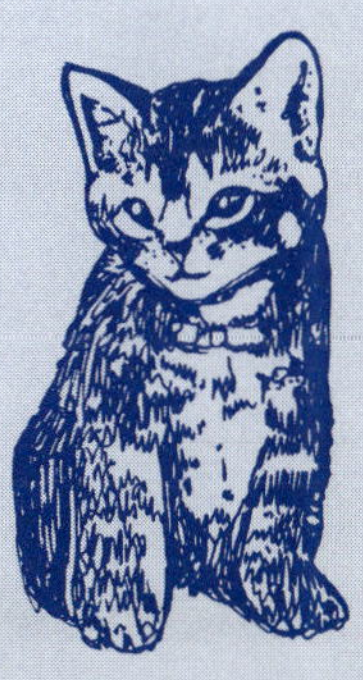

Some female cats, as they age, get like old, beloved aunties, full of love.

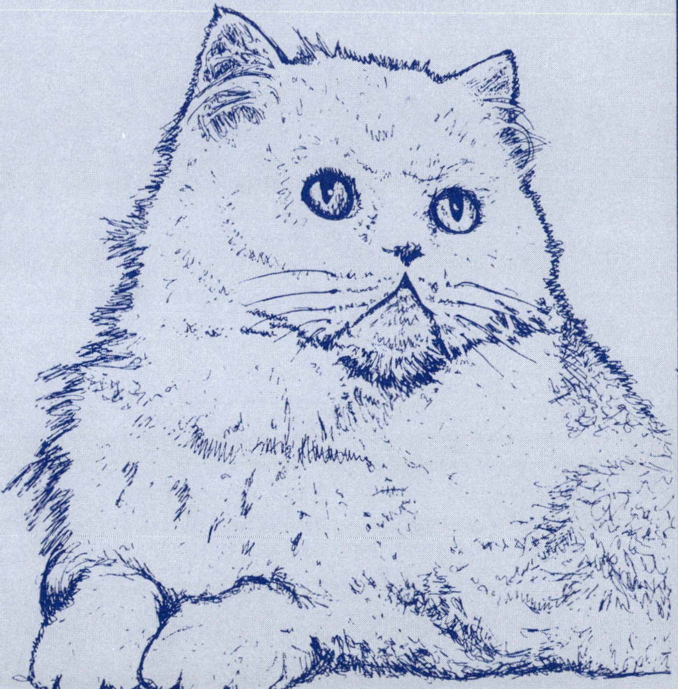

I think you grow richer by the amount of love you give to people or to animals. I mean—you get to be a better person and a happier one. It's hard to love a cat whom you know will die before you do; but the years spent with Susie, the years spent with Tamar, with Sherpa, were all worth it.

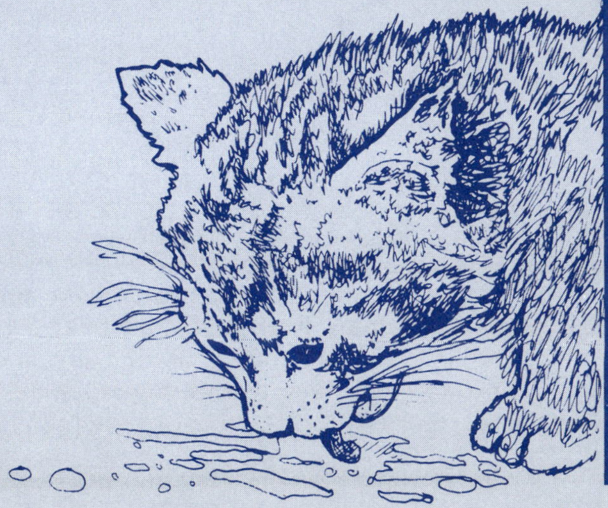

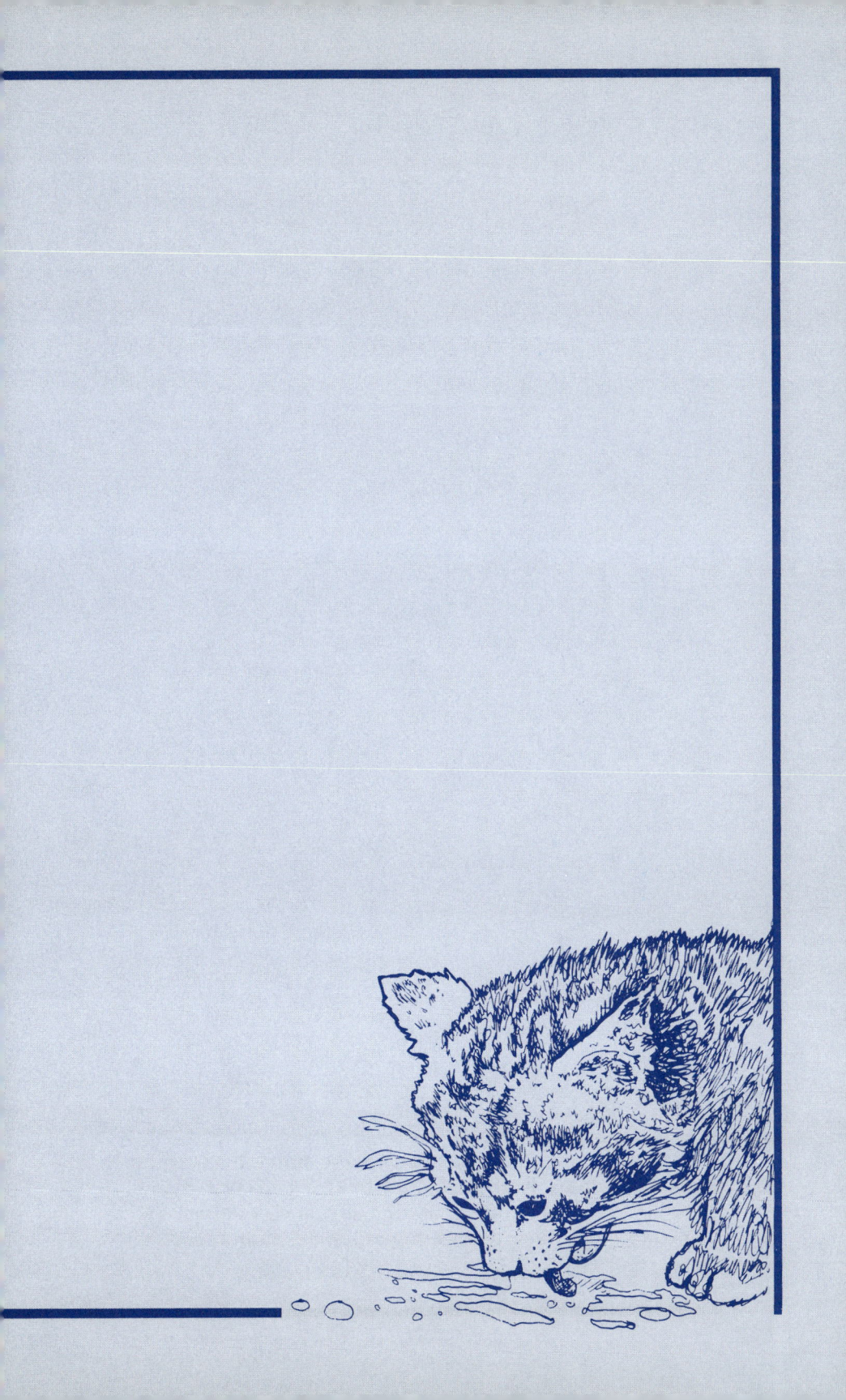

I've tried to save several kittens that were either given up by their mothers or lost on the street and obviously close to dying. It almost never works out to try and save a sick animal. It's better to pay attention to a healthy kitten or cat and reap the rewards.

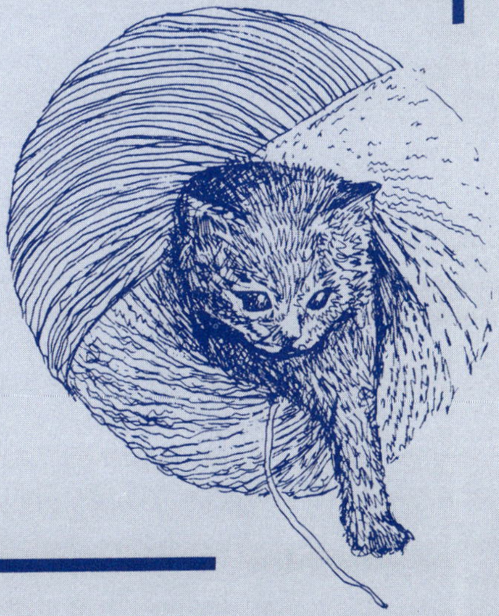

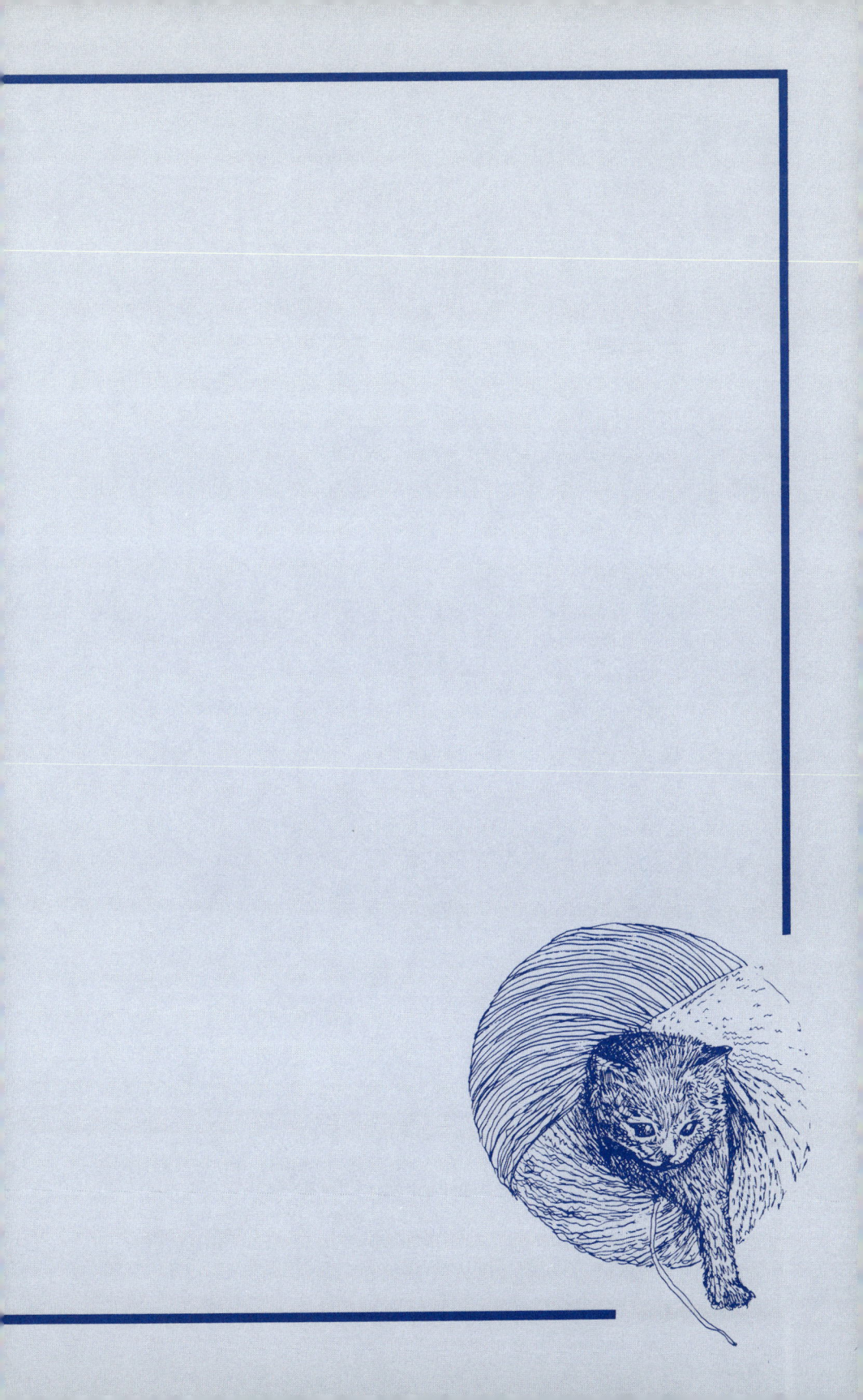

Cats do take long journeys. Sherpa has gone on seven to eight mile trips, over streams, across highways, to get back to a house or something he wanted. He always came back if what he wanted wasn't there or if he couldn't find it. I have respect for the endurance and independence of cats.

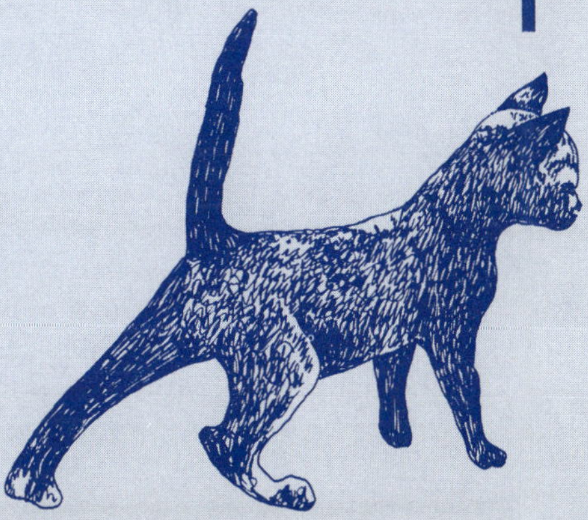

Kittens don't have too much sense about cars. If you have a kitten running around loose near your car, or if you don't know where a kitten is, please check near the tires (on the top) and under the car before you move the car.

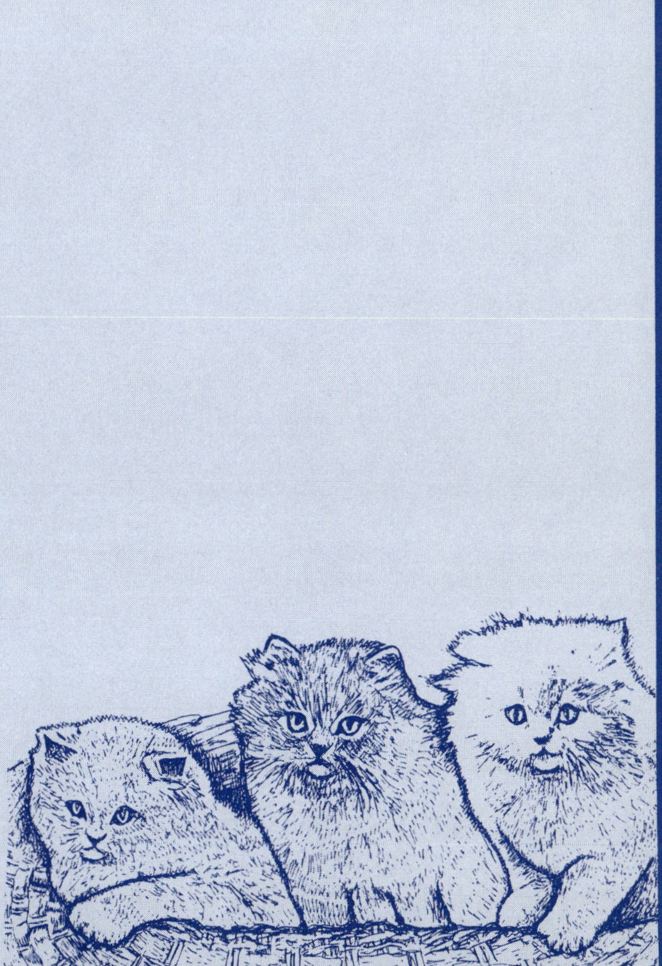

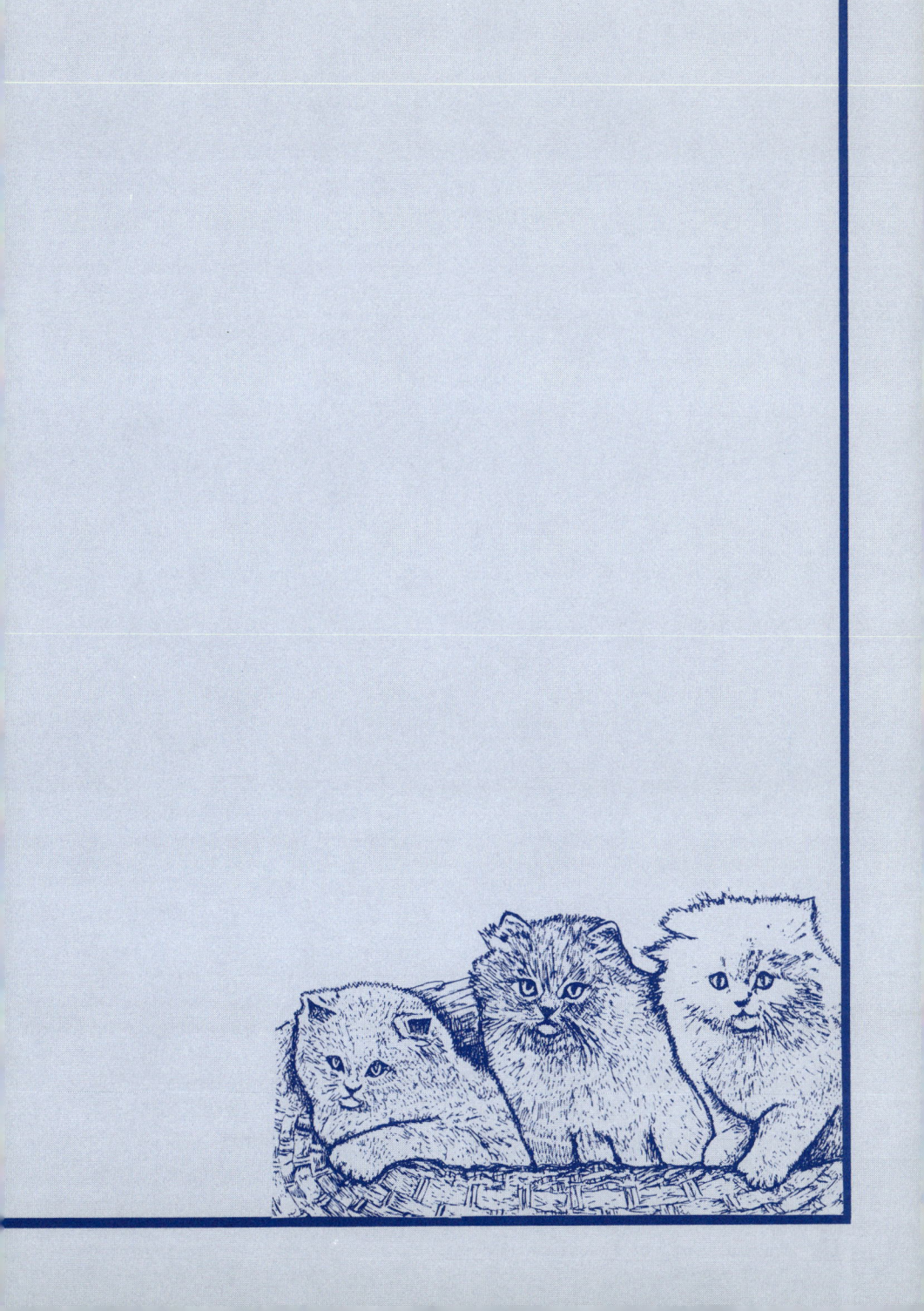

I also wouldn't let young cats out at night. I once came across two grey kittens sitting in the middle of the street. There was no moon and I couldn't distinguish them from the black road. I braked just in time.

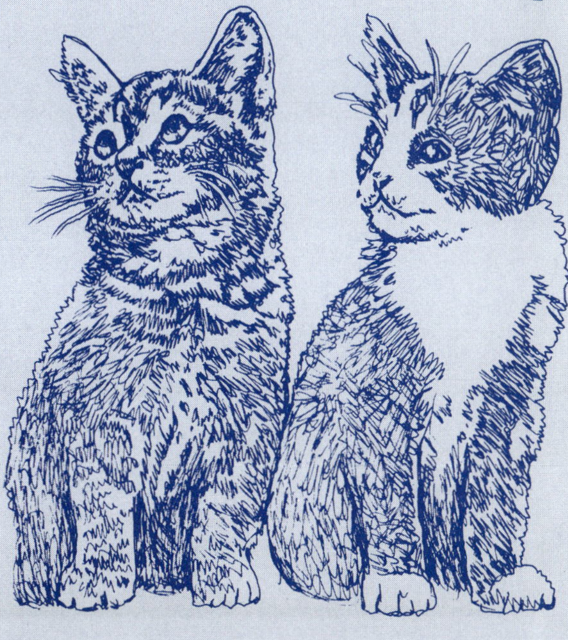

Most cats can't survive falls from high places. Be careful of open windows. Put a sturdy screen between the cat and the air outside, or leave the window open only two inches.

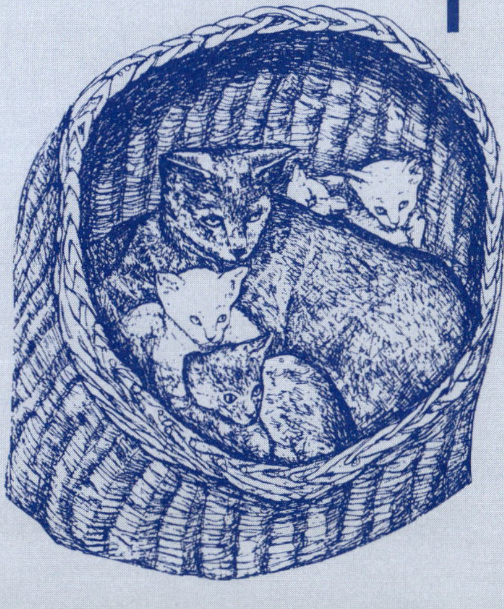

My Abyssinian, in a burst of love, would often bite me tenderly on the nose. I've known cats to suck on their owner's ear lobes.

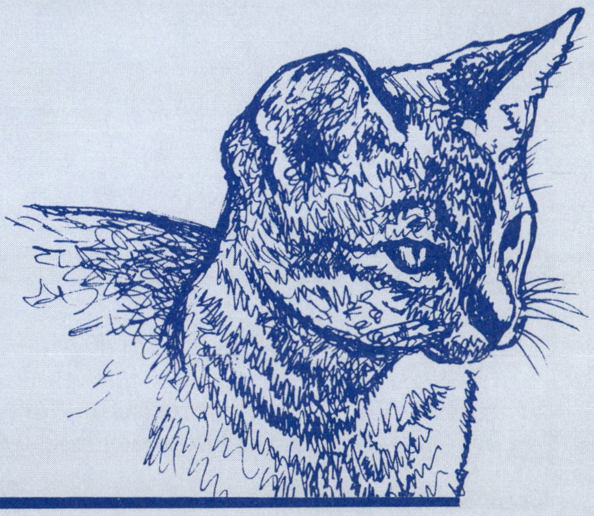

When we lived in the country and went for a walk at night with the dogs, Sherpa would go with us trailing us, often for miles. His endurance wasn't as great as the dogs, and sometimes we'd have to carry him the last stretch back to the house.

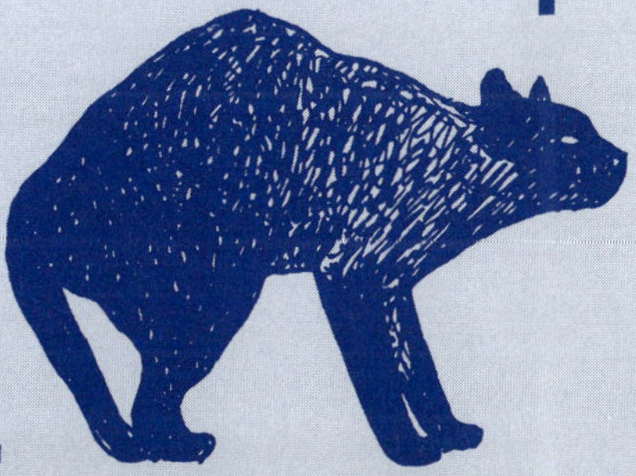

Sherpa also tried to follow us when we walked the dog at night in Santa Cruz, but in the city we thought it too dangerous and used to put him in the car and close it up carefully. Actually, he found the car a very comfortable place to sleep.

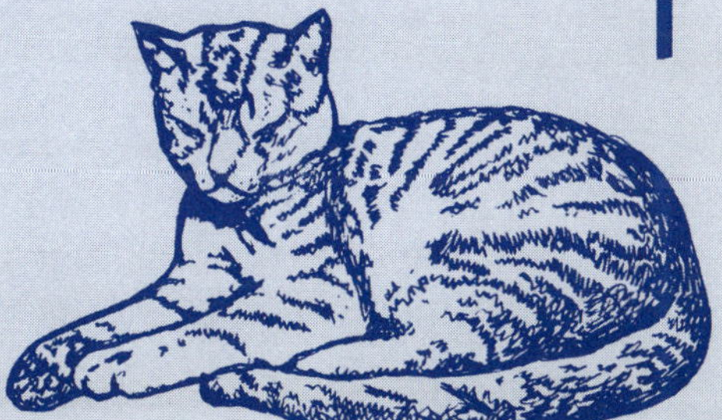

Cats that are fed regularly will probably be good mousers. My Abyssinian was the best hunter we ever had. Either the skill is taught by the mother or maybe it's genetically inherited.

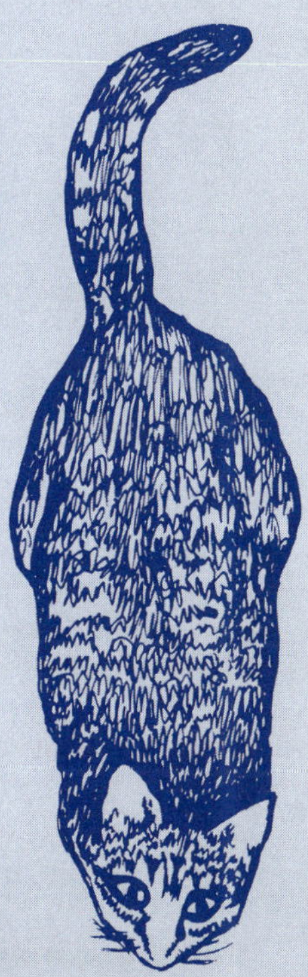

I honestly have never met a cat I didn't like, but, yes, there was one, Cody, whom I could never figure out. He was my son's girlfriend's cat. He never had any sort of relationship with me. I mean, he didn't give a damn. He was a one-woman cat, and I wasn't it.

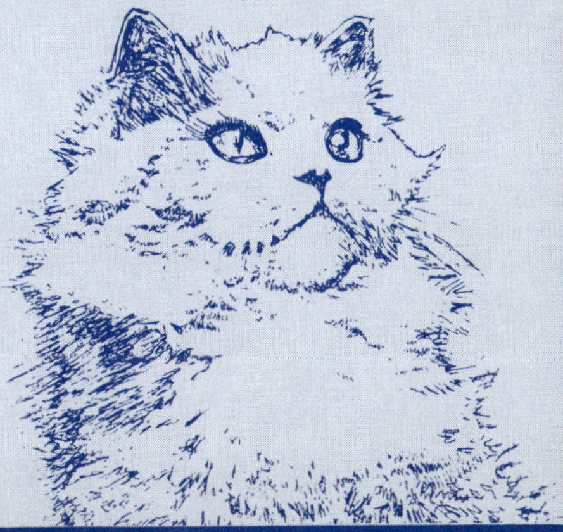

There's no greater pleasure than having a cat sit on your lap, warm and contented.

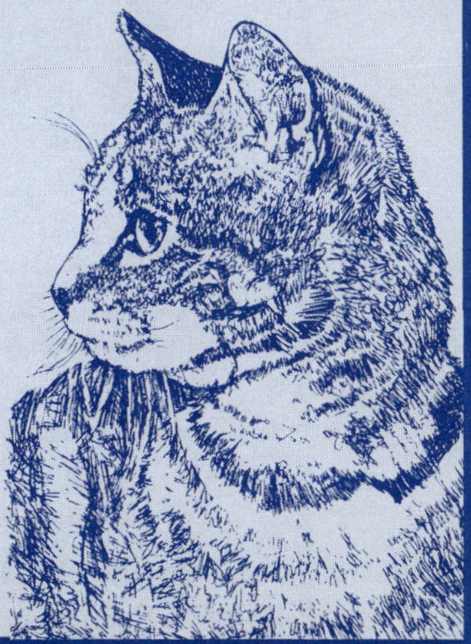

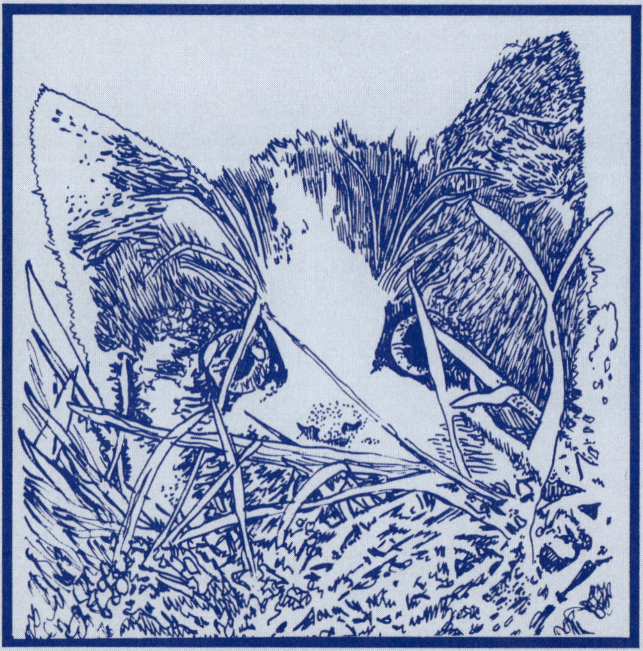